COMBINATION MICROWAVE COOKERY

HAMLYN

Published by The Hamlyn Publishing Group Limited,
a division of The Octopus Publishing Group
Michelin House, 81 Fulham Road, London SW3 6RB

First published 1988

Photographs taken from The Octopus Publishing Group
copyright publications 1979–1987.

Additional photography by David Jordan

The publishers would like to thank G.F. Smith & Son,
London, Ltd. for permission to use their Parch Marque
papers as background colours in this book.

ISBN 0 600 55764 2

Typeset in Bembo by Servis Filmsetting Limited,
Manchester
Printed by Mandarin Offset, Hong Kong

Contents

Introduction

Combination Microwave Cooking

Combination cooking is the method of cooking using microwave energy and conventional heat simultaneously. The majority of ovens offering this facility combine the microwave energy with recirculating hot air, produced by the high-speed fan built into the oven. Take all the time-tested standards of traditional cooking and marry them with the speed of cooking with microwaves: the result is the best of good cooking with the advantages of modern technology.

In the recipes in this book the microwave power setting and the temperature setting are given in conjunction with one another in the method. The temperature is given in degrees centigrade (C) only to conform with the settings on the ovens that are available. (In the recipes in which microwave energy only is used, this is clearly indicated in the method.)

The range of cooking temperatures that can be selected varies according to the different ovens; however, it is usually in the region of 140–250 c. The microwave settings that can be used in combination with heat also vary from oven to oven. The majority of ovens allow for the use of high, medium, or low microwave settings in combination with conventional heat. Some models limit the use of microwave settings to medium when using the combination cooking mode and other ovens offer high or low microwave settings. The majority of combination cooking is carried out on a medium microwave setting.

By using microwaves the cooking process is speeded up and by using conventional heat the food turns brown and develops a crisp texture, or crust. Cooking by microwaves alone produces food with a steamed flavour. However, cooking by the combination method results in food which has a baked flavour.

Pastry, 'roast' meat and batters are a few examples of foods that are inferior or unacceptable when cooked by microwaves only. Cook these items by a combination of microwaves and conventional heat and the results are excellent – pastry becomes crisp, flaked and tasty with a brown crust; meat roasts very well, giving a traditional result in significantly less time than roasting by conventional means; and batters rise, become crisp and turn brown in a fraction of the time normally taken.

Breads and cakes rise too, cook through and have a crisp, browned crust. The taste is similar to that achieved by conventional methods.

Any recipes that require the food to be thoroughly heated or cooked through, with a crisp coating or browned topping are also particularly successful in the combination oven. While the crisp coating, or pastry pie lid, cooks and browns the food underneath cooks through without drying out.

Microwave Cooking

All combination cookers can be used to cook by microwaves only. Any power setting available can be selected and the results will be the same as those achieved in any other standard microwave cooker. Remember always to read the manufacturer's instructions and to follow them.

Microwave cooking is a fast, moist cooking method, ideal for vegetables, fish, rice, sauces, soups, certain meat dishes and poultry. The microwaves excite the water molecules in food, causing friction which in turn creates heat. Because of the speed of cooking, tough cuts of meat do not cook successfully. The moist characteristic of this cooking method does not give a crust, so any foods that rely on the formation of a crust for successful cooking cannot be cooked by microwaves alone. Choux pastry, soufflés and batters are examples of recipes that cannot be cooked successfully by microwaves alone.

Convection cooking

The great advantage of the combination cooker is that you can use it on the convection mode to cook all your own favourite recipes. Convection cooking uses conventional heat that is recirculated in the oven by means of a fan. The movement of the hot air within the oven cavity speeds up the cooking process. The air moves around the food, rapidly displacing the cold air from the uncooked food. The result is not only speedy cooking, but even heat distribution (and cooking) throughout the oven.

The effect of cooking in a fan-assisted oven is equivalent to about 20 c hotter than the actual setting selected. So, if you put something in to cook at 180 c, because of the recirculated air, the cooking time is equivalent to that required at 200 c in a normal oven. If you are cooking something that requires slow cooking, then reduce the setting accordingly; otherwise reduce the cooking time.

Cooking Utensils

When using microwaves only do not use metal cooking containers. Avoid any dishes that have metal trims, metal clips and ties or any metal utensils. The exceptions to the no-metal rule when cooking in the microwave only mode are small pieces of cooking foil, used to shield small areas of food that are in danger of overcooking. In some cases, it is possible to use small foil containers when the majority of the foil area is covered by food. The rule is *follow the manufacturer's instructions.*

Use ovenproof glassware, specially produced plastics and ovenproof china. Most household china is suitable for microwave cooking, some earthenware is useful (although it may absorb a certain amount of microwave energy) and basketware can be used for short-term heating using microwaves only.

Cover food during cooking if it is likely to dry out – use a lid, a plate or special microwave cling film. *Do not use ordinary plastic film.* Roasting bags are suitable for use in the microwave oven – but don't forget to avoid metal ties.

All the basic rules of microwave cooking apply to the combination method. Although many of the manufacturers suggest that baking tins can be used in combination ovens (a special insulating mat is sometimes provided) the microwaves do not pass through the metal so the use of ovenproof dishes is recommended for best results.

Remember that the oven does become hot when using the combination mode so always have oven gloves ready to remove dishes when the food is cooked.

Microwave settings

The following power levels apply to the different settings used in the recipes. In testing on combination mode little difference in cooking time was evident between 600W and 650W.

- ◆ HIGH   600W or 650W
- ◆ MEDIUM   350W or 360W
- ◆ LOW   180W

Temperature settings

- ◆ The temperature settings given in the recipes go up to 250 C.
- ◆ If the maximum temperature for your oven is 240 C, then use it instead of 250 C.
- ◆ If your oven has a limited number of temperature settings, then select the one nearest to the temperature given in the recipe. If necessary, use a lower temperature than that suggested instead of a hotter setting.

Soups and Starters

Microwave cooking is an ideal method for stocks and soups. The starters show how well this method works in combination with conventional heat, apart from the Smoked Haddock Mousse, which is cooked using microwaves only.

CHICKEN STOCK

MAKES 900 ml/1½ PINTS

**1 large chicken joint
bay leaf · sprig of thyme
2 parsley sprigs · 2 carrots, sliced
1 celery stick, sliced · 1 onion, chopped
900 ml/1½ pints boiling water
salt and freshly ground black pepper**

Put the chicken joint in a large casserole dish. Add the herbs and vegetables. Pour in 300 ml/½ pint of the water and cover. Cook, using microwaves only, on high for 10 minutes. Pour in the remaining boiling water and leave to stand for 15 minutes.

Strain, setting aside the chicken and squeezing all the juice out of the vegetables. Discard the chicken skin, dice all the meat and add to the stock. (Alternatively, reserve the chicken for another use.) Add seasoning to taste. Use as required, as a base for soups, sauces and casseroles.

BEEF STOCK

MAKES 900 ml/1½ PINTS

**100 g/4 oz lean bacon, chopped
225 g/8 oz lean minced beef
1 large onion, chopped
2 large carrots, chopped · bay leaf
large parsley sprig · sprig of thyme
900 ml/1½ pints boiling water
salt and freshly ground black pepper**

Put the bacon, beef and vegetables in a casserole dish with the herbs. Pour in 600 ml/1 pint of the boiling water and cover. Cook, using microwaves only, on high for 10 minutes, stir well, cook for a further 5 minutes. Pour in the remaining boiling water and leave to stand for 15 minutes.

Strain the stock, pressing all the goodness out of the ingredients. Taste and adjust the seasoning as necessary. Use in stews, soups and sauces.

TOMATO AND MUSHROOM SOUP

SERVES 4

**1 large leek, trimmed, sliced and washed
1 large onion, chopped
1 clove garlic, crushed
25 g/1 oz butter
900 ml/1½ pints Chicken Stock (this page)
1 teaspoon wine vinegar
8 ripe tomatoes, chopped
2 tablespoons tomato purée
225 g/8 oz button mushrooms, diced
bouquet garni
salt and freshly ground black pepper**

Garnish
**4 button mushrooms, sliced
chopped parsley**

Put the leek, onion, garlic and butter in a large casserole dish or mixing bowl and cover. Cook on high for 3 minutes. Pour in 300 ml/½ pint of the stock, add the wine vinegar, tomatoes, tomato purée, mushrooms and bouquet garni and cover.

Cook, using microwaves only, on high for 10 minutes, stir well, then cook for a further 10 minutes. Remove the bouquet garni, blend the soup in a liquidiser until smooth, then sieve to remove the tomato seeds. Return the soup to the casserole dish or bowl. Stir in the remaining stock and season. Cook, uncovered, for 5–8 minutes.

Serve the soup garnished with mushroom slices and chopped parsley. Accompany with fresh vegetable crudités as shown, if liked.

SPICY VEGETABLE SOUP

SERVES 4

1 large onion, chopped
1 large potato, diced
3 celery sticks, sliced
1 large parsnip, diced
25 g/1 oz butter
900 ml/1½ pints Chicken Stock (page 6)
2 tablespoons tomato purée
generous pinch of oregano
pinch of ground cumin
1 teaspoon prepared French mustard
salt and freshly ground black pepper

Garnish
paprika
sprigs of mint

Put the onion, potato, celery, parsnip and butter in a large casserole dish or bowl. Cover, then cook, using microwaves only, on high for 7 minutes. Pour in 300 ml/½ pint of the stock, then add the tomato purée, oregano, cumin, mustard and seasoning.

Cook on high for 10 minutes, stir well, then cook for a further 10 minutes. Stir in the remaining stock and season to taste. Cook, uncovered, for 5–8 minutes, then serve garnished with a sprinkling of paprika and mint sprigs.

Top: Tomato and Mushroom Soup; *bottom*: Spicy Vegetable Soup

SEAFOOD GRATINS

SERVES 4

3 tablespoons plain flour
1 bay leaf
blade of mace
300 ml/½ pint milk
salt and freshly ground white pepper
25 g/1 oz butter
50–75 g/2–3 oz Cheddar cheese, grated
175 g/6 oz white fish fillet, skinned and cubed
4 scallops, cleaned and sliced, or 100 g/4 oz
** peeled cooked prawns**

Topping
25 g/1 oz fresh breadcrumbs
50 g/2 oz Cheddar cheese, grated

To make the cheese sauce, place the flour in a large basin with the bay leaf and mace. Gradually pour in the milk, whisking all the time to prevent the flour from forming lumps. Add seasoning to taste and the butter, then cook, using microwaves only, on high for 3–4 minutes. Whisk thoroughly, then add the cheese, whisk well, then cook on high for a further 10 minutes, until the sauce has boiled and thickened. Whisk well to remove any lumps, then taste and adjust the seasoning.

Add the seafood to the sauce, mix in thoroughly, then divide the mixture between four small dishes or large ramekins. Mix the breadcrumbs with the cheese and sprinkle on top. Bake at 250 C using medium microwave setting for 7–8 minutes, or until golden brown.

Variation
To turn this recipe into a main meal, boil about 1 kg/2 lb potatoes by the conventional method, then drain and mash with butter and milk, seasoning with pepper to taste. Follow the recipe for Seafood Gratins, but double the recipe quantities given. Pipe the prepared potato round the edge of a shallow ovenproof dish and fill the middle with the fish mixture. Bake at 220 C using medium microwave setting for 13–15 minutes, until lightly browned on top.

DEVILLED MACKEREL

SERVES 4

2 medium mackerel, filleted
100 g/4 oz low-fat soft cheese, for example,
    quark, sieved cottage cheese or curd cheese
4 tablespoons soured cream
1 tablespoon wholegrain mustard
dash of Worcestershire sauce
1 tablespoon horseradish sauce
salt and freshly ground black pepper
75 g/3 oz Cheddar cheese, finely grated
25 g/1 oz fresh breadcrumbs
parsley sprigs to garnish

Skin the mackerel fillets and flake the fish into large pieces. Mix with the soft cheese, soured cream, seasonings and 50 g/2 oz of the Cheddar. Oil four individual ramekins and put in the mackerel mixture. Mix the breadcrumbs with the remaining Cheddar and sprinkle on top of the fish mixture.

Bake at 250 c using medium microwave setting for 8 minutes. Serve garnished with parsley sprigs.

FISH PATTIES

SERVES 4

Bacon-coated fish cakes are exceptionally tasty and they cook very well in the combination microwave. The chopped bacon in the coating yields just enough fat to ensure that the result is crisp and as good as if it were fried.

225 g/8 oz potatoes, grated
2 tablespoons lemon juice
350 g/12 oz white fish, skinned and diced
100 g/4 oz fine fresh breadcrumbs
1 tablespoon chopped parsley
salt and freshly ground black pepper
1 egg
1 tablespoon cold water
100 g/4 oz rindless streaky bacon, chopped
25 g/1 oz plain flour

Yogurt Sauce
1 tablespoon chopped mixed herbs
4 tablespoons mayonnaise
150 ml/¼ pint natural yogurt

Garnish
lemon wedges
watercress sprigs

Put the potato in a basin with the lemon juice, cover and cook, using microwaves only, on high for 8 minutes. Immediately stir in the fish, half the quantity of breadcrumbs, parsley and seasoning to taste and mix thoroughly. Form the mixture into four patties.

Lightly oil a flan dish. Beat the egg with the water; mix the bacon with the remaining breadcrumbs. Coat the fish patties first in the flour, then dip in the beaten egg. Coat thoroughly in the bacon mixture, pressing it on well, and place the patties in the prepared flan dish. Cook at 250 c using medium microwave setting for 8 minutes on one side. Turn the patties over and cook for a further 4 minutes on the other side.

Meanwhile, to make the sauce, stir the herbs into the mayonnaise, mix in the yogurt and season to taste.

Arrange the fish cakes on a serving dish and garnish with lemon wedges and watercress sprigs. Serve immediately with the sauce poured over.

SAVOURY PEAR PACKETS

SERVES 4

1 (370-g/13-oz) packet puff pastry
175 g/6 oz blue cheese, finely crumbled
50 g/2 oz full-fat soft cheese
1 tablespoon finely chopped onion
4 pears
juice of 1 lemon
beaten egg or milk to glaze

Heat the oven to 220 c. Roll out the pastry to a 30-cm/12-in square. From this cut four 8.5-cm/3½-in rounds. Use the remainder to cut pastry strips 2.5 cm/1 in wide.

Prepare the filling for the pears by mixing the blue cheese, full-fat soft cheese and onion together. Peel the pears and remove the core from underneath. Brush with lemon juice. Stuff the cored pears with the filling and place on the rounds of pastry. Dampen the pastry strips with water, then wind around the pears, overlapping the pastry rounds. The strips should be well sealed together and should completely cover the pears. Use any remaining pastry to make leaves to decorate the tops of the pears.

Brush with beaten egg or milk, place on a flan dish and bake at 220 c using medium microwave setting for 10 minutes.

COURGETTE PUFFS WITH DERBY DRESSING

MAKES 16

1 medium courgette
1 (250-g/8.82-oz) packet puff pastry,
    defrosted if frozen
a little beaten egg
olive oil to brush

Dressing
100 g/4 oz Sage Derby cheese, finely grated
150 ml/¼ pint natural yogurt
1 tablespoon chopped chives

Heat the oven to 220 c. Trim the courgette and cut it into 16 slices. Roll out the pastry to a 25 × 50-cm/10 × 20-in rectangle. Cut the pastry into 32 6-cm/2½-in squares.

Place each courgette slice on a pastry square, dampen the edges of the pastry with beaten egg and place a second pastry square on top. Seal the edges. When all 16 squares are complete, brush each one with a little olive oil. Lightly grease a flan dish and bake the puffs in two batches, at 220 c using medium microwave setting, for 6 minutes per batch.

To make the cheese dressing, mash the Sage Derby with the yogurt until creamy. Add the chives and chill. Alternatively, blend the cheese with the yogurt in a liquidiser until smooth, add the chives and chill. Serve the courgette puffs hot or warm with the dressing.

DUCK PÂTÉ

SERVES 6

1 onion, chopped
25 g/1 oz butter
225 g/8 oz pork, minced
2 boneless duck breasts, skinned
and finely diced or minced
pinch of ground mace
pinch of grated nutmeg
salt and freshly ground black pepper
2 tablespoons brandy
grated rind and juice of 1 orange
1 egg, beaten
75 g/3 oz fresh breadcrumbs

Garnish
orange slices
aspic

Place the onion and butter in a 15-cm/6-in round soufflé dish, or similar round ovenproof dish, cover and cook, using microwaves only, on high for 3 minutes. Add the minced pork and the diced or minced duck. Cover and cook for a further 5 minutes, stirring once.

Mix in all the remaining ingredients, then cook at 200 c using medium microwave setting for 15 minutes.

Press the pâté with a small saucer and a heavy weight on top of it until cool. Chill, still weighted, for several hours before serving. Garnish with orange and aspic before serving.

Aspic
Packets of aspic jelly are available from some supermarkets and delicatessens. Dissolve the aspic powder in 150 ml/$\frac{1}{4}$ pint water in a basin, using microwaves only, on high for 1–1$\frac{1}{2}$ minutes, or until very hot but not boiling. Stir well, then make up to the quantity suggested on the packet instructions using cold water.

SMOKED HADDOCK MOUSSE

SERVES 4–6

225 g/8 oz smoked haddock fillet
1 tablespoon water
15 g/½ oz powdered gelatine
150 ml/¼ pint chicken stock
1¼ tablespoons lemon juice
75 g/3 oz Gouda cheese, grated
freshly ground black pepper
75 g/3 oz butter
1 tablespoon chopped parsley

Garnish
lemon wedges · cucumber slices
tomato wedges · mustard and cress

Place the haddock in a dish with the water. Cover and cook, using microwaves only, on high for 3–3½ minutes. Allow to cool slightly. Mix the gelatine with the stock and leave to soften for 2 minutes. Cook, using microwaves only, on high for 1 minute until the gelatine is clear and dissolved.

Flake the haddock and blend in a liquidiser with the gelatine, lemon juice, cheese and pepper to taste until smooth. Place the butter in a bowl and heat, using microwaves only, on high for 1¼ minutes to melt. Stir into the haddock mixture with the parsley, blending well. Pour into a small greased ring mould and chill until set.

To serve, dip the mould briefly into hot water and turn the mousse on to a serving plate. Garnish as shown.

GAMMON COCOTTES

SERVES 4

350 g/12 oz gammon steak
1 small onion, chopped
1 tablespoon plain flour
150 ml/¼ pint milk
freshly ground black pepper
100 g/4 oz button mushrooms, sliced

Garnish
parsley sprigs · croûtons (see Note)

Trim the fat off the gammon, then cut the meat into small cubes. Place in a shallow dish (a flan dish is ideal) with the onion. Cook at 250 c using medium microwave setting for 8 minutes.

Stir in the flour, milk and seasoning. Add the mushrooms and cook, using microwaves only, on high for 3 minutes, or until the sauce is slightly thickened. Divide between four individual dishes, garnish with parsley and croûtons and serve.

Microwave Croûtons
Cut sliced bread into tiny cubes, discarding the crusts if you like. Place the cubes on a piece of absorbent kitchen paper on a plate. Cover with a second piece of paper and cook, using microwaves only, on high. For 4 slices of bread allow about 4–6 minutes, until the bread is really dry and crisp.

Melt some butter in a small basin, adding chopped herbs and/or garlic, if you like. Allow about 30–60 seconds on high for the butter. Toss the croûtons in the butter, leave for a minute or two, then drain on absorbent kitchen paper.

Fish Dishes

This chapter makes full use of the combination mode and, in addition, includes information at the end about cooking fish using microwaves only, as well as incorporating a guide to cooking fish and shellfish.

MUSTARD MACKEREL

SERVES 4

4 small mackerel, cleaned and heads removed
salt and freshly ground black pepper
4 teaspoons French mustard
juice of ½ lemon
25 g/1 oz butter

Garnish
tomato slices
lemon slices
parsley sprigs

Rinse the fish and dry the body cavities well. Season and spread the inside of each mackerel with a teaspoon of mustard. Place the fish in a large shallow dish, then sprinkle with the lemon juice and dot with the butter.

Cook at 250 c using medium microwave setting for 7–9 minutes. Transfer the mackerel to a serving dish, pour over the cooking juices and serve garnished with tomato and lemon slices and parsley sprigs.

COD STEAKS WITH PEPPERS AND ONIONS

SERVES 4

4 (175–225 g/6–8 oz) cod steaks
25 g/1 oz butter
1 green pepper, deseeded and sliced into rings
1 onion, sliced
150 ml/¼ pint soured cream, or natural yogurt
salt and freshly ground black pepper

Put the steaks in a buttered shallow dish, then dot with half the quantity of butter. Cook at 220 c using medium microwave setting for 6–7 minutes. Cover and set aside to keep hot.

Put the green pepper and onion rings in a basin with the remaining butter, cover and cook, using microwaves only, on high for 5–7 minutes, until tender. Add the soured cream or yogurt, season to taste, then cook for a further 1 minute. Pour the sauce over the fish steaks and serve.

Variation
For a delicious alternative topping for cod steaks try the following combination: slice 225 g/8 oz courgettes and put the slices in a large basin with 25 g/1 oz butter. Cover and cook, using microwaves only, on high for 2 minutes. Add 2 trimmed and chopped spring onions to the courgette slices, cover, then cook, using microwaves only, on high for a further 2 minutes. Stir in 1 (400-g/14-oz) can of chopped tomatoes, seasoning to taste, and ½ teaspoon of chopped fresh thyme or rosemary, if you like. Re-cover the basin and cook, using microwaves only, on high for a further 3–4 minutes.

Top: Mustard Mackerel; *bottom*: Cod Steaks with Peppers and Onion

COULIBIAC

SERVES 4–6

1 onion, finely chopped
75 g/3 oz long-grain rice
300 ml/½ pint boiling water
2 hard-boiled eggs
1 (213-g/7½-oz) can salmon
100 g/4 oz frozen peas
50 g/2 oz button mushrooms, sliced
salt and freshly ground black pepper
1 (370-g/13-oz) packet puff pastry, defrosted
  if frozen
1 egg, beaten

Put the onion, rice and water in a large basin, cover with a plate or special microwave cling film and cook, using microwaves only, on high for 10 minutes. Leave to cool. Heat the oven to 250c. Stir all the remaining ingredients, except the pastry and beaten egg, into the rice.

On a lightly floured work surface roll out the pastry into a 30 × 38-cm/12 × 15-in rectangle. Place the rice and salmon mixture down the centre of the pastry and brush the pastry edges with a little beaten egg. Fold over the sides and ends of the pastry and press the edges together firmly to seal in the filling. Carefully lift the coulibiac on to a large flan dish so that the pastry join is underneath. Cut three diagonal slashes on the top, and brush with beaten egg to glaze.

Bake at 250c using medium microwave setting for 8–10 minutes, or until the pastry is well puffed and browned. Serve hot or cold, following the serving suggestion in the photograph, if liked. Soured cream spooned on to individual portions is a delicious accompaniment.

STUFFED COD STEAKS

SERVES 4

100 g/4 oz potatoes, grated
½ small onion, chopped
2 tablespoons milk
25 g/1 oz fresh breadcrumbs
salt and freshly ground black pepper
4 (175–225 g/6–8 oz) cod steaks
2 tomatoes (optional)
15 g/½ oz butter
2 teaspoons cornflour
4 tablespoons fish stock, dry cider,
    white wine, or water
150 ml/¼ pint single cream
2 tablespoons chopped parsley

Put the potato in a basin with the onion and milk. Cover and cook, using microwaves only, on high for 7 minutes, stirring once. Heat the oven to 200 c.

Add the breadcrumbs and seasoning to the potato and onion and mix well. Arrange the cod steaks in a shallow dish, then stuff them with the potato mixture. Cut the tomatoes into eight slices, if using, and arrange two slices on each piece of fish. Dot with the butter and bake at 200 c using medium microwave setting for 8–10 minutes, or until the fish is cooked and the filling is lightly browned.

To make a parsley sauce for the cod, blend the cornflour with the stock, cider, wine or water in a basin. Add the cream and cook, using microwaves only, on high for 3–4 minutes until thickened. Stir in the parsley and season to taste. Serve the fish with the sauce poured over.

FISH FLORENTINE

SERVES 4

1 (198-g/7-oz) can tuna in oil
1 onion, chopped
3 tablespoons plain flour
300 ml/½ pint milk
salt and freshly ground black pepper
100 g/4 oz mushrooms, sliced
450 g/1 lb frozen spinach
100 g/4 oz Cheddar cheese, grated
50 g/2 oz breadcrumbs

Drain the oil from the tuna into a basin. Add the onion and cook, using microwaves only, on high for 3 minutes. Whisk in the flour and milk. Cook for 3–4 minutes, then add the tuna, seasoning and mushrooms.

Place the spinach in a gratin dish and cook, using microwaves only, on high for 5 minutes or until defrosted. Drain off any excess liquid, squeezing the spinach lightly with the back of a spoon. Spread out evenly, then top with the tuna sauce. Mix the cheese and breadcrumbs. Sprinkle over the top and bake at 200c using medium microwave setting for 8 minutes, until browned and crisp.

LATTICE TUNA TART

SERVES 4

175 g/6 oz plain flour
pinch of salt
75 g/3 oz margarine
2 tablespoons water
beaten egg

Filling
1 (198-g/7-oz) can tuna in oil
1 onion, chopped
2 tablespoons plain flour
150 ml/¼ pint milk
1 (326-g/11½-oz) can sweetcorn, drained

Sift the flour and salt into a bowl. Cut the margarine into small pieces and rub into the flour until the mixture resembles fine breadcrumbs. Add sufficient water to mixture to make a short dough.

Drain the oil from the tuna into a basin, add the onion and cook, using microwaves only, on high for 3 minutes. Stir in the 2 tablespoons flour and the milk. Cook, using microwaves only, on high for 2 minutes. Stir in the tuna and sweetcorn.

Roll out just over half the pastry and use to line a 20-cm/8-in pie plate. Prick the pastry all over and chill. Roll out the remaining pastry into a rectangle, about 20 × 15 cm/8 × 6 in, and cut it into narrow strips. Cook the pastry base at 220c using medium microwave setting for 2–3 minutes. Spread the filling over the pastry, then arrange the pastry strips over the filling. Brush with beaten egg. Bake the tart at 220c using medium microwave setting for 7–8 minutes.

From the top: Fish Florentine; Lattice Tuna Tart; Fish Pie
(*page 20*)

FISH PIE

SERVES 4–6

1.5 kg/3 lb potatoes, diced
4 tablespoons water
1 onion, chopped
75 g/3 oz butter
salt and freshly ground black pepper
3 tablespoons plain flour
300 ml/½ pint milk
1 bay leaf
675 g/1½ lb white fish fillet, skinned, for
    example, cod, haddock or coley
100 g/4 oz mushrooms, sliced

Place the potato in a large bowl with the water. Cover with special microwave cling film, allowing a small gap for the steam to escape, then cook, using microwaves only, on high for 20–25 minutes. Allow the potato to stand in the bowl while you begin to prepare the filling.

Place the onion in a bowl with 25 g/1 oz of the butter and cook, using microwaves only, on high for 3 minutes. Add the remaining butter to the potato and mash, adding seasoning to taste.

Stir the flour into the onion, then add the milk and season to taste. Stir in the bay leaf, fish and mushroom and cook, using microwaves only, on high for 13 minutes, stirring once during cooking. Taste and adjust the seasoning.

Top the fish with the mashed potato and brown under a hot grill. Allow to stand for a minute before serving.

Combination microwave alternative

For a brown, crunchy crust on the potato topping, cook the pie using microwaves and conventional heat in combination.

Prepare the potatoes as above. Cook the onion and butter, then stir in the flour, milk, seasoning and bay leaf and cook, using microwaves only, on high for 3 minutes. Stir well, then stir in the fish and top with the potato.

Cook at 200 c using high microwave setting for 5 minutes, then continue to cook at 200 c using medium-high microwave setting for a further 8–10 minutes, until well browned on top.

COOKING FISH USING MICROWAVES ONLY

Fish, with its delicate, tender flesh requires minimum cooking and is cooked very successfully using microwaves only. Whole fish, fillets, steaks and chunks of fish can be cooked in an infinite number of ways. They can be cooked with just a knob of butter and seasoning or fresh herbs, in a rich or simple sauce, in breadcrumbs or cream. Some general points to observe when cooking fish steaks and whole fish are made below, while a guide to cooking specific types of fish is provided opposite.

To cook fish steaks

Place the fish steaks in a dish, tucking in any flaps to make a neat shape and securing with wooden cocktail sticks if necessary. Add water and lemon juice as recommended or brush with a lemon butter mixture. If liked, the dish can be lined with absorbent kitchen paper before cooking the fish. Cover tightly with special microwave cling film, then either turn back the corner or snip two holes in the top to allow the steam to escape. Cook for half the recommended time. If the dish is lined with absorbent kitchen paper turn the steaks over and re-cover; alternatively, if absorbent kitchen paper is not used, give the dish a half turn. Cook for the remaining time, or until the fish flakes easily.

To cook whole fish

Place the fish in the dish and brush with a sauce, butter or add water as recommended. Shield and protect the head and the tail area with a little foil. Slash the skin two or three times to prevent it from bursting during cooking. Cover lightly with special microwave cling film and turn back one corner or snip two holes in the top to allow the steam to escape. Cook for the recommended time.

Guide to cooking fish using microwaves only

Fish		Quantity	Cooking time in minutes on high	Preparation
Bass	whole	450 g/1 lb	5–7	Shield the head and tail with foil. Cut the skin in two or three places to prevent it from bursting.
Cod	fillets	450 g/1 lb	5–7	Place the fillet tails to the centre of the dish or shield with foil. Cut the skin in two or three places to prevent it from bursting.
	steaks	450 g/1 lb	4–5	Cover with greaseproof paper before cooking.
Haddock	fillets	450 g/1 lb	5–7	Place the fillet tails to the centre of the dish or shield with foil. Cut the skin in two or three places to prevent it from bursting.
	steaks	450 g/1 lb	4–5	Cover with greaseproof paper before cooking.
Halibut	steaks	450 g/1 lb	4–5	Cover with greaseproof paper before cooking.
Kippers	whole	1	1–2	Cover with special microwave cling film and snip two holes in the top to allow the steam to escape.
Red Mullet and Red Snapper	whole	450 g/1 lb	5–7	Shield the head and tail with foil. Cut the skin in two or three places to prevent it from bursting.
Salmon	steaks	450 g/1 lb	4–5	Cover with greaseproof paper before cooking.
Salmon Trout	whole	450 g/1 lb	7–8	Shield the head and tail with foil. Cut the skin in two or three places to prevent it from bursting.
Scallops		450 g/1 lb	5–7	Cover with dampened absorbent kitchen paper.
Smoked Haddock	whole	450 g/1 lb	4–5	Cover with special microwave cling film, snipping two holes in the top to allow the steam to escape.
Trout	whole	450 g/1 lb	8–9	Shield the head and tail with foil. Cut the skin in two or three places to prevent it from bursting.

Guide to reheating boiled shellfish

Shellfish		Quantity	Cooking time in minutes on high	Preparation
Lobster	tails	450 g/1 lb	5–6	Turn tails over halfway through the cooking time.
	whole	450 g/1 lb	6–8	Allow to stand for 5 minutes before serving. Turn over halfway through the cooking time.
Prawns and Scampi		450 g/1 lb	5–6	Arrange the peeled shellfish in a ring in a shallow dish and cover with special microwave cling film, snipping two holes in the top to allow the steam to escape.
Shrimps		450 g/1 lb	5–6	Arrange the peeled shrimps in a ring in a shallow dish and cover with special microwave cling film, snipping two holes in the top to allow the steam to escape.

Poultry and Meat

ROAST TURKEY

SERVES 8

1 (4.5-kg/10-lb) oven-ready turkey

Stuffing
25 g/1 oz butter
1 large onion, chopped
3 celery sticks, chopped
175 g/6 oz dry white breadcrumbs
grated rind of $\frac{1}{2}$ lemon
1$\frac{1}{2}$ tablespoons lemon juice
grated rind of 1 orange
4 tablespoons orange juice
1 (175-g/6-oz) jar cranberry sauce
2 teaspoons dried mixed herbs
salt and freshly ground black pepper
1 egg, beaten

Garnish
bacon rolls (optional)
watercress sprigs

To make the stuffing, put the butter in a large basin with the onion and celery and cover. Cook, using microwaves only, on high for 5 minutes. Stir the breadcrumbs, lemon rind and juice, orange rind and juice, cranberry sauce, herbs and salt and pepper to taste, into the onion and celery. Mix well and bind the ingredients with the beaten egg.

Stuff the turkey with the mixture. Use a trussing needle or large darning needle and buttonhole thread to secure the stuffing. Place breast-uppermost in a large flan dish.

Roast at 200 c using medium microwave setting for 30 minutes. Turn the turkey over, drain off any excess fat and cook for a further 30 minutes. Turn the turkey again so that the breast is uppermost and cook for a final 15–20 minutes, or until the meat is cooked through. Test whether the turkey is cooked by piercing it at the thickest part – there should be no sign of any pink meat and the juices should run clear.

Leave to stand for 15 minutes, then serve hot, with a garnish of bacon rolls, if liked, and watercress sprigs. Alternatively, the turkey can be served cold.

BONED STUFFED CHICKEN

SERVES 4–6

1 (1.5-kg/3-lb) oven-ready chicken
1 small onion, chopped
50 g/2 oz butter
350 g/12 oz lean minced pork
40 g/1½ oz fresh breadcrumbs
2 eggs, beaten
½ teaspoon tarragon
salt and freshly ground black pepper
225 g/8 oz chicken livers, trimmed
watercress sprigs to garnish

Trim the leg and wing ends of the chicken. To bone the chicken, place it breast-side down on a large clean work surface. Using a sharp, pointed knife, cut straight down the middle of the back, from head to tail. Working on one side, cut off all the meat, as near to the bone as possible. Take time and use the point of the knife to cut the meat away from the bones. Take great care not to puncture the skin. When you come to the leg and wing, carefully scrape the meat down the joints. As you near the ends of the joints, turn the meat and skin inside out to leave the bones completely cleaned. Carefully work round underneath the breast meat, cleaning the ribs as far as the main breast bone. Now leave the first side and remove the meat from the second side in the same way.

When you reach the breast bone, very carefully cut the finest sliver of bone off to separate the carcass completely from the meat without cutting the skin at all. The bones can be used along with the giblets to make an excellent stock.

To prepare the stuffings, put the onion in a bowl with 15 g/½ oz butter and cook, using microwaves only, on high for 3 minutes. Stir the pork, breadcrumbs, eggs and tarragon into the onion, seasoning well. Put the chicken livers in a bowl with 25 g/1 oz butter and cook, using microwaves only, on high for 4–5 minutes, until almost cooked.

Lay the boned chicken, skin-side down, flat on the surface. Spread half the pork mixture down the centre of the chicken. Spread the chicken livers evenly over the pork mixture, then cover with the remaining pork mixture. Carefully lift the sides of the chicken over the stuffings to enclose them.

Using a trussing needle or large darning needle and buttonhole thread, sew up the bird, then turn it over so that the breast meat is uppermost. Press it into a neat shape, tucking the wing and leg ends underneath and plumping up the middle. Place in a large flan dish and dot with the remaining butter.

Roast at 220 c using medium microwave setting for 20–25 minutes; turn the chicken over halfway through cooking. Serve hot or cold, sliced.

DUCK WITH CHERRY SAUCE

SERVES 4

1 (1.75–2-kg/4–4½-lb) oven-ready duck
salt and freshly ground black pepper

Sauce
2 tablespoons plain flour
300 ml/½ pint stock (made from the duck
   giblets, or chicken stock)
225 g/8 oz canned black cherries,
   drained and stoned

Trim any excess fat from the duck. Prick the skin all over with a fork, then season well inside and out. Place the duck breast-uppermost in a flan dish or any flat dish that fits into the oven.

Cook at 250 c using medium microwave setting for 10 minutes. Turn the duck over and drain off any excess fat if necessary. Cook for a further 10 minutes. Again, drain off any fat which is likely to overflow from the dish, turn the duck over so that the breast is uppermost. Cook for a final 10–12 minutes. The skin should be crisp and browned. Pierce the duck at the thickest point. The juices should be free of blood when the bird is cooked. Transfer the duck to a heated serving dish. Cover with foil, placing the shiny side inwards to reflect the heat back towards the bird. Do not wrap the bird tightly or the skin will lose its crisp texture.

Drain the fat from the cooking dish, reserving the juices. Stir in the flour, then gradually whisk in the stock. Stir in the cherries. If you find the dish awkward to lift when full of liquid, then pour the sauce ingredients into a basin, making sure that all the goodness is scraped off the dish. Cook, using microwaves only, on high for 3–5 minutes, or until the sauce is boiling. Taste and adjust the seasoning. Serve the duck with the sauce poured around it, as in the picture. Alternatively, the duck may be carved beforehand and arranged in slices with the sauce.

TOMATO CHICKEN CASSEROLE

SERVES 4

1 onion, halved and sliced
25 g/1 oz butter
1 clove garlic, crushed
100 g/4 oz mushrooms, sliced
1 (400-g/14-oz) can chopped tomatoes
½ teaspoon marjoram
salt and freshly ground black pepper
300 ml/½ pint boiling chicken stock
4 chicken quarters

Place the onion, butter and garlic in a casserole and cook, using microwaves only, on high for 3 minutes. Stir in the mushrooms, tomatoes, marjoram, seasoning and stock.

Arrange the chicken joints on top of the sauce, skin-side down. Cook at 250c using high microwave setting for 7 minutes. Turn the joints over and reduce the temperature to 200c, then cook using medium microwave setting for a further 10–12 minutes, until the chicken is cooked through.

SPICED CHICKEN

SERVES 4

1 large onion, chopped
2 cloves garlic, crushed
1 celery stick
2 tablespoons oil
¼ teaspoon chilli powder
½ teaspoon ground ginger
1 (400-g/14-oz) can chopped tomatoes
salt and freshly ground black pepper
4 chicken quarters

Place the onion, garlic, celery and oil in a casserole dish and cook, using microwaves only, on high for 4 minutes. Stir in the chilli powder, ginger, tomatoes and seasoning. Place the chicken on top, skin-side down.

Cook at 250c using high microwave setting for 7 minutes. Turn the joints over and continue to cook at 250c using medium microwave setting for 10–12 minutes.

CHICKEN JAMBOREE

SERVES 4

This glaze is also good for brushing over chicken pieces when barbecuing.

1 tablespoon white or red wine vinegar
3 tablespoons redcurrant jelly
grated rind and juice of 1 orange
50 g/2 oz raisins
pinch of curry powder
4 chicken joints

Put all the ingredients, except the chicken joints, in a basin. Cover and cook, using microwaves only, on high for 45–60 seconds.

Place the chicken joints, skin-side down, in a flan dish. Pour the prepared glaze over the top, then cook at 250 c using high microwave setting for 5 minutes. Turn over the chicken joints and cook for a further 15 minutes, making sure that the glaze is evenly spooned over the chicken.

STUFFED LAMB

SERVES 6

75 g/3 oz fresh breadcrumbs
1 onion, chopped
2 cloves garlic, crushed
2 tablespoons chopped parsley
salt and freshly ground black pepper
50 ml/2 fl oz stock
1 (1.5-kg/3-lb) shoulder of lamb, boned
watercress sprigs to garnish (optional)

Rich Wine Sauce
2 tablespoons plain flour
150 ml/$\frac{1}{4}$ pint boiling water
300 ml/$\frac{1}{2}$ pint full-bodied red wine
1 tablespoon tomato purée
generous dash of Worcestershire sauce

Mix together the breadcrumbs, onion, garlic, parsley and seasoning, and stir in a little stock to give a crumbly texture. Use a spoon to press this mixture into the lamb. Use a trussing or darning needle and strong thread to sew up the lamb and seal in the stuffing.

Place the lamb on a large flan dish and roast at 200 c using medium microwave setting for 20

minutes. Turn the lamb over and continue to cook for 15 minutes. Turn the lamb again and cook for a final 10 minutes. Each time you turn the lamb, check to make sure that there is no danger of fat spilling over.

Wrap the cooked lamb in foil, shiny side inwards. Drain off excess fat and stir the flour into the cooking juices. Stir in the boiling water and wine, then whisk in the tomato purée and Worcestershire sauce. Cook, using microwaves only, on high for 5 minutes, whisk well and taste. Adjust the seasoning, then cook for a further 2–3 minutes, or until the sauce is boiling and slightly thickened.

Transfer the lamb to a serving dish and garnish with watercress, if liked. Serve the sauce separately. Remember to remove the thread as you carve the lamb.

BAKED LIVER

SERVES 4

450 g/1 lb lamb's liver, trimmed and sliced
beef stock cube
300 ml/½ pint boiling water
1 small onion, chopped
15 g/½ oz butter
25 g/1 oz fresh breadcrumbs
½ teaspoon grated lemon rind
salt and freshly ground black pepper
4 rindless rashers bacon
parsley sprigs to garnish

Put the liver slices in a suitable dish. Crumble in the stock cube, and pour in the boiling water. Cook, using microwaves only, on high for 5 minutes. Rearrange the liver, putting the cooked slices to the centre of the dish.

Cook the onion in a basin with the butter, using microwaves only, on high for 3 minutes. Add the breadcrumbs and lemon rind; season to taste and mix well, then sprinkle the mixture over the liver. Bake at 220c using medium microwave setting for 5 minutes. Arrange the bacon rashers on top of the liver and cook for a further 10 minutes. Serve freshly cooked with parsley sprigs to garnish.

LAMB ANNA

SERVES 4

1 small onion, chopped
25 g/1 oz butter
100 g/4 oz pork sausagemeat
1 egg, beaten
100 g/4 oz breadcrumbs
½ teaspoon dried mixed herbs
½ teaspoon French mustard
salt and freshly ground black pepper
1 (675-g/1½-lb) breast of lamb, boned and
    trimmed of excess fat

Vegetable Base
1 large potato, peeled and diced
2 carrots, peeled and sliced
1 parsnip, peeled and diced
1 turnip, peeled and diced
1 onion, chopped
2 tablespoons plain flour
300 ml/½ pint beef stock

To make the stuffing, put the onion in a basin with the butter and cook, using microwaves only, on high for 3 minutes. Stir in the sausagemeat, egg, breadcrumbs, herbs, mustard and salt and pepper to combine the ingredients thoroughly.

Toss all the vegetables with the flour in a large shallow dish or casserole. Pour in half of the stock, cover and cook, using microwaves only, on high for 10–12 minutes, until almost tender. Stir well.

Cut across the width of the lamb breast, then spread each piece with the stuffing and roll up. Tie neatly. Pour the remaining stock over the vegetables. Place the meat on top and cook at 220 c using medium microwave setting for 20–25 minutes, turning the meat over after 10 minutes cooking time. The lamb looks best if it is sliced before serving.

ITALIAN NOISETTES

SERVES 4

1 green pepper
1 red pepper
1 large onion, sliced
1 clove garlic, crushed
2 tablespoons olive oil
1 (400-g/14-oz) can chopped tomatoes
100 g/4 oz courgettes, sliced
salt and freshly ground black pepper
8 noisettes of lamb

Cut the tops off the peppers, remove the core and seeds and slice the shells. Place in an ovenproof casserole dish with the onion, garlic and olive oil.

Cook, using microwaves only, on high for 5 minutes. Add the tomatoes, courgettes and seasoning and cook for a further 2 minutes.

Arrange the noisettes of lamb on top of the vegetables and cook at 220 c using medium microwave setting for 18–20 minutes, turning the pieces of lamb over halfway through the cooking time.

PORK WITH ORANGE

SERVES 6

1 large onion, thinly sliced
25 g/1 oz butter
grated rind and chopped fruit of 2 large
    oranges
4 digestive biscuits, crushed
salt and freshly ground black pepper
1.5 kg/3 lb loin of pork, boned
a little oil · 1 tablespoon brown sugar
$\frac{1}{4}$ teaspoon ground coriander

Garnish
orange slices · lettuce hearts
watercress sprigs

For the onion and orange stuffing, put the onion
and butter in a basin and cook, using microwaves
only, on high for 3 minutes. Stir in the orange rind
and fruit, biscuit crumbs and salt and pepper.

Lay the meat flat and spread over the stuffing.
Roll up and tie with string. Score the rind, rub
with oil, salt, the sugar and coriander and place the
pork in a dish, rind uppermost. Cook at 220 c
using medium microwave setting for 15 minutes,
then reduce the temperature to 190 c and cook for
a further 30 minutes. Baste the pork frequently,
and turn twice during cooking time. For the final
5 minutes cooking time increase the temperature
to 220 c and cook with rind uppermost. Leave to
stand for 5–10 minutes before serving.

STUFFED ROAST PORK
WITH CRANBERRY
APPLES

SERVES 8

1 (2.25-kg/5-lb) leg of pork, boned
salt
1 tablespoon oil

Stuffing
2 large onions, chopped
15 g/$\frac{1}{2}$ oz butter
2 tablespoons chopped fresh sage
50 g/2 oz fresh white breadcrumbs
salt and freshly ground black pepper
milk to bind

Cranberry Apples
8 dessert apples
8 tablespoons cranberry sauce
4 tablespoons cold water
25 g/1 oz butter

Gravy
3–4 tablespoons plain flour
600 ml/1 pint boiling chicken stock, or
300 ml/$\frac{1}{2}$ pint chicken stock and
300 ml/$\frac{1}{2}$ pint wine
salt and freshly ground black pepper

Rub the pork rind with salt and score well. Place the onion in a basin with the butter. Cook, using microwaves only, on high for 3 minutes. Mix in the sage, breadcrumbs, salt and pepper to taste, and sufficient milk to bind the stuffing ingredients together.

Insert the stuffing into the bone cavity of the pork and tie the joint firmly. Place in a dish and drizzle the oil over the meat. Roast the pork at 220 c using medium microwave setting for 5 minutes. Reduce the temperature to 180 c using medium microwave setting and cook for a further 60 minutes, basting frequently and turning the meat twice during the cooking time.

While the meat is cooking, wipe the apples but do not peel them. Core the fruit and score the skin halfway down, circling the apples completely. Arrange the apples in a greased flan dish and fill each one with a tablespoon of cranberry sauce. Sprinkle over the water. Cut the butter into small flakes and put on top of the apples.

Transfer the cooked meat to a warm serving dish and cover with foil, retaining the cooking juices for the gravy. Cook the apples at 180 c using medium microwave setting for 7 minutes.

To make the gravy, drain excess fat from the meat juices, then stir in the flour. Whisk in the chicken stock, or combination of stock and wine. Season to taste and cook, using microwaves only, on high for 10 minutes. Whisk well.

Remove the foil from the meat, arrange the apples around the joint and serve with the gravy and vegetables of your choice.

COTTAGE PIE

SERVES 4

1 kg/2 lb potatoes, cut into small chunks
4 tablespoons water
1 large onion, sliced
2 tablespoons oil
50 g/2 oz butter
about 50 ml/2 fl oz milk
salt and freshly ground black pepper
350 g/12 oz minced beef
2 tablespoons plain flour
1 teaspoon dried mixed herbs
300 ml/$\frac{1}{2}$ pint boiling beef stock, or 1 stock
    cube dissolved in 300 ml/$\frac{1}{2}$ pint boiling
    water
2 tomatoes, peeled and sliced

Place the potato in a large bowl with the water. Cover with special microwave cling film, allowing a small gap for the steam to escape, then cook, using microwaves only, on high for 15–18 minutes, stirring once during the cooking time.

Put the onion and oil in a large casserole dish or suitable ovenproof serving dish. Cook, using microwaves only, on high for 3 minutes.

Meanwhile, mash the potato thoroughly with the butter and milk, adding salt and pepper to taste. Stir the beef into the onion, breaking up the meat well and seasoning to taste. Stir in the flour and herbs, then pour in the stock, or stock cube dissolved in the boiling water. Add the tomato slices, and cook the meat mixture, using microwaves only, on high for 5 minutes.

Cover the meat with the mashed potato, marking the surface with a fork. Bake the Cottage Pie at 250 c using medium microwave setting for 10 minutes, or until the potato topping is golden brown, then serve immediately with a seasonal vegetable accompaniment.

BAKED GAMMON

SERVES 6–8

1.5–1.75-kg/3$\frac{1}{2}$–4-lb gammon joint
blade of mace
bay leaf
about 150 ml/$\frac{1}{4}$ pint dry cider or water
cloves
2 tablespoons honey

Garnish (optional)
pineapple rings
glacé cherries

Put the gammon joint in a large casserole dish or mixing bowl. Add the mace and bay leaf, then pour in enough cider or water to come about one-third of the way up the joint. The quantity of liquid will depend on the size and shape of the casserole dish.

Cover and cook at 200 c using medium microwave setting for 20 minutes. Turn the joint over and re-cover, then cook for a further 20 minutes. Reduce the oven temperature to 180 c and continue to cook using medium microwave setting for 10–15 minutes. Pierce the gammon underneath to check that it is almost cooked.

Remove the joint, discarding the cooking liquid (or reserve it to flavour a soup or stew), and cut off the rind. Mark the fat into diamond shapes. Insert cloves between the diamonds and put the joint back into the casserole. Brush the honey over the gammon and cook at 180 c using medium microwave setting for a final 10 minutes. Leave to stand for 15 minutes before serving, garnished with pineapple rings and glacé cherries, if liked.

Clockwise from bottom left: Cottage Pie; Baked Gammon; Lancashire Hot Pot

LANCASHIRE HOT POT

SERVES 4

1 leek, trimmed, sliced and washed
2 medium carrots, sliced
1 turnip, cut into cubes
1 onion, chopped
50 g/2 oz butter
1 kg/2 lb best end of neck of lamb, chopped
  into pieces
2 tablespoons plain flour
salt and freshly ground black pepper
bay leaf
sprig of thyme
parsley sprig
600 ml/1 pint boiling water
675 g/1½ lb potatoes, sliced

Put the wet leek, carrot, turnip and onion into a basin with half the quantity of butter, cover and cook, using microwaves only, on high for 5 minutes.

Trim any excess fat off the meat. Put the pieces in a polythene bag, then sprinkle in the flour and plenty of seasoning. Shake the bag well to coat the meat in the seasoned flour. Put the meat in a large casserole dish, adding any leftover flour. Add the herbs and vegetables, then pour in the boiling water. Top with the potato, overlapping the slices.

Dot with the remaining butter and cook, using microwaves only, on high for 10 minutes. Continue cooking at 220 c using medium microwave setting for 25–30 minutes, or until the meat is tender and the potato crisp and brown.

STEAK BOULANGÈRE

SERVES 4

800 g/1¾ lb potatoes, thinly sliced
1 onion, chopped
2 tablespoons water
4 (225–350-g/8–12-oz) rump steaks
75 g/3 oz butter
1 small clove garlic, crushed
1 tablespoon chopped parsley
1 tablespoon lemon juice

Layer the potato and onion in a large flan dish and sprinkle with the water. Cover and cook, using microwaves only, on high for 8 minutes, rearranging the potato halfway through the cooking time.

Meanwhile, make the garlic butter by creaming the butter, garlic, parsley and lemon juice together.

Arrange the steaks on top of the potato, overlapping them to fit. Dot with the garlic butter, then cook at 250 c using medium microwave setting for 10–12 minutes.

MEAT ROASTING CHART

Meat	Micro-wave power setting	Temp-erature °C	Minutes per 450 g/1 lb	Instructions Note: No need to preheat oven for cooking times over 30 minutes.
BEEF				
Rump Steak –medium/ well done	Medium	240–250	5–6	Preheat oven. Brush steak with a little oil and place on rack or in a large shallow dish. Turn halfway.
Rump Steak –well done	Medium	240–250	7–8	As above.
Topside/ Sirloin	Medium	180	12–15	Place joint in dish or on rack. Turn and baste twice during cooking.
Rolled Rib	Medium	180	12–15	As above.
Rib on the Bone	Medium	180	10–12	Turn joint and baste once or twice during cooking.
Brisket	Medium	220–180	14–15	Place meat on bed of diced vegetables (onion, carrot and potato). Add 150–300 ml/¼–½ pint water and season. Cook at 220 for 15 minutes, then reduce temperature for remaining time. Turn twice during cooking.
LAMB				
Chops	Medium	240–250	7–9	Preheat oven. Arrange chops in dish, sprinkle with herbs. Turn over halfway through cooking.
Steaks (Slices off the leg)	Medium	240–250	10–12	As above.
Leg	Medium	190	9–11	Season the joint and place in a dish. Turn and baste two or three times during cooking.
Shoulder	Medium	200	10–12	As above.
Breast, boned and rolled	Medium	220	13–14	As above.
PORK				
Chops	Medium	240–250	7–9	Preheat oven. Arrange in dish and season. Turn halfway through cooking.
Loin, boned and rolled	Medium	220–190	14–16	Score rind, rub with salt and place pork in dish. Reduce temperature after 15 minutes. Baste frequently, turn twice, having rind uppermost for 5 minutes at the end of cooking time. Increase temperature again for last 5 minutes. Leave to stand for 5–10 minutes before serving.
Loin, on the bone	Medium	220–190	15–16	Score rind and rub with salt. Place pork in dish, rind uppermost. Cook as above, reducing temperature after 5 minutes. Increase temperature at the end of cooking if the rind needs crisping.
Leg	Medium	220–180	15–16	Rub rind with salt and score well. Place in dish. Reduce temperature after 5 minutes. Baste frequently, turn twice during cooking.
Pork Belly	Medium	240–250	10	Score rind, rub with salt. Place in dish and turn twice during cooking. Have rind uppermost to start, underneath for the majority of cooking, then on top for final 3–5 minutes.
GAMMON	Medium	200–180	15–18	Place in deep casserole or mixing bowl. Add chopped onion, carrot and bay leaf. Pour in 300–600 ml/½–1 pint boiling water. Cover. Turn joint twice during cooking. Reduce temperature halfway through cooking. Leave to stand for 15 minutes.

MEAT SAUCE

SERVES 4

The microwave is excellent for making a tasty meat sauce, which forms the perfect complement for many pasta shapes. Use the sauce to top spaghetti as Spaghetti Bolognese, for example, or make it the basis of a Lasagne baked by combination microwaves. Spaghetti is best cooked conventionally in plenty of boiling salted water, but follow our method for perfect Lasagne.

1 onion
2 cloves garlic, crushed
2 tablespoons oil
450 g/1 lb lean minced beef
50 g/2 oz mushrooms, sliced
2 tablespoons tomato purée
1 (400-g/14-oz) can tomatoes
salt and freshly ground black pepper
2 teaspoons marjoram
150 ml/¼ pint beef stock
150 ml/¼ pint red wine

Place the onion and garlic in a large basin with the oil. Cover and cook, using microwaves only, on high for 5 minutes. Stir in the meat, breaking up the mince as you do so, the tomato purée, tomatoes, seasoning and marjoram, then pour in the stock and wine. Stir thoroughly, cover and cook for 15 minutes, stirring once during cooking time.

LASAGNE SPECIAL

SERVES 4

225 g/8 oz lasagne
1 quantity meat sauce (above)
100 g/4 oz cream cheese
50 g/2 oz Parmesan cheese, grated
100–150 g/4–5 oz Gruyère cheese, thinly sliced

Cook the lasagne in plenty of boiling salted water on top of the hob for about 20 minutes, until just tender. Drain and rinse well under cold running water, then separate the sheets and lay them on a double thickness of absorbent kitchen paper.

Put a layer of lasagne into a buttered dish, then add a layer of meat sauce. Follow with a little cream cheese, Gruyère and Parmesan, and continue to layer the ingredients, as shown in the picture, ending with layers of Parmesan and Gruyère. Cook at 250 c using medium microwave setting for 15 minutes. Serve at once.

Vegetable Dishes

Both microwave only and combination modes are given for baking potatoes, so why not try both and see which you like best? As vegetables cook successfully by microwaves only, this method is employed for most of the remaining recipes.

BAKED POTATOES MICROWAVES ONLY

Here are times for cooking potatoes using microwaves only on high. Large potatoes are big enough to make a meal in themselves, and medium baked potatoes could be served as an accompaniment to a main dish. One of these would make an average portion, while two would be a really generous helping. The potatoes should be pricked with a fork before cooking, otherwise they may burst.

Cooking times
Large (275–350-g/10–12-oz) potatoes

1 potato	8 minutes
2 potatoes	15 minutes
4 potatoes	27 minutes

During cooking, there should be no need to turn one or two potatoes but the four potatoes would need rearranging once or twice.

Medium (150–175-g/5–6-oz) potatoes

1 potato	4 minutes
2 potatoes	5–6 minutes
4 potatoes	10 minutes
6 potatoes	18–19 minutes

During cooking the six potatoes would require rearranging once, smaller numbers should not need moving round.

When the potatoes are cooked, brush them with a little oil or butter and put them under a hot grill for a few minutes, turning them once, to make the skin crisp and brown. This is not essential, but if you like crisp skins this is the way to achieve them.

COMBINATION MICROWAVE METHOD

For the combination microwave alternative cooking method, brush the potatoes with a little oil and place straight on the rack (or on a flat dish on the rack). Cook at 250c using high microwave setting. Cooked using conventional heat as well as microwaves, the skin becomes crisp and browned.

Cooking times
Large (275–350-g/10–12-oz) potatoes

1 potato	7 minutes
2 potatoes	10 minutes
3 potatoes	18 minutes
4 potatoes	25 minutes
5 potatoes	28–30 minutes
6 potatoes	35 minutes

BAKED POTATO TOPPINGS

Soured Cream and Chives
Stir 2 tablespoons chopped chives into 150 ml/$\frac{1}{4}$ pint soured cream.

Soured Cream with Anchovy
Mash 1 (50-g/2-oz) can anchovy fillets with the oil from the can. Add seasoning to taste and 150 ml/$\frac{1}{4}$ pint soured cream.

Cream Cheese with Pineapple
Mix 1 (340-g/12-oz) can pineapple pieces (drained of juice) into 225 g/8 oz cream cheese.

Cream Cheese with Ham and Onion
Finely chop 100 g/4 oz cooked ham and 4 spring onions, then mix these ingredients into 225 g/8 oz cream cheese.

Cream Cheese and Salami
Beat a little single cream into the cream cheese to make it thin enough to pipe. Fold sliced salami into cornets, then pipe a little cream cheese into each. Arrange two salami cornets on each slit potato with tomato wedges and parsley.

Lemon Prawns
Cook 1 small chopped onion with 25 g/1 oz butter, using microwaves only, on high for 5 minutes. Add 225 g/8 oz peeled cooked prawns and the grated rind of 1 lemon. Heat for 2 minutes on high, then spoon on to the potatoes.

BAKED POTATO STUFFINGS

Savoury Stuffed Potatoes

Allow 50 g/2 oz grated cheese for each potato and add 1 tablespoon grated onion for each. Mash the potato with butter, seasoning and milk, then mix in the cheese, onion, plenty of chopped parsley and 25 g/1 oz chopped cooked ham for each potato. Pile back into the skins and heat under the grill to serve.

Fisherman's Potatoes

Thoroughly mash 1 (120-g/4¼-oz) can sardines in tomato sauce with seasoning to taste, 1 crushed garlic clove, a little lemon rind and a dash of Worcestershire sauce. Mix into the potato mashed with butter and spoon the filling into the skins. Top with grated cheese and grill until golden.

Porky Potatoes

Finely chop 2 freshly cooked pork sausages for each potato. Mash the potato with butter, a pinch of rubbed sage and plenty of chopped parsley. Stir in the sausage and pile the potato back into the shells. Top with parsley or sage sprigs and serve.

BAKED POTATO FILLINGS

For the following ideas, you will need large potatoes. Cut the baked potatoes in half and scoop out the middle of the potatoes. Mash the potato with butter, milk and seasoning, then put it back into the skins, pressing it against the sides and piling it up round the edge. If you like the potato mixture can be piped back into the skins, but this is difficult if you are not used to handling very hot piping bags. The mashed potato case should be browned under a hot grill before the filling is added.

Greek Salad Potatoes

An unusual but delicious combination of creamy hot potato and very crunchy cold salad. Allow a little diced cucumber, a little chopped onion and green pepper, 1 small tomato, peeled, deseeded and chopped and 50 g/2 oz crumbled feta cheese for each potato. Mix all these salad ingredients and dress them with a little olive oil. Pile them into the potato and add a few black olives.

Potato Scrambles

Prepare the potatoes, then, when they are under the grill browning, scramble the required number of eggs (about 2 to each potato). Top with chopped parsley and a couple of slices of tomato.

CRUMBLY BUTTERED BRUSSELS

SERVES 4

450 g/1 lb Brussels sprouts, trimmed
4 tablespoons water
salt
75 g/3 oz butter
1 clove garlic, crushed (optional)
6 tablespoons freshly toasted
  breadcrumbs
pinch of cayenne

Place the sprouts in a large dish with the water and a pinch of salt. Cover and cook, using microwaves only, on high for 7–9 minutes, stirring once. Drain thoroughly.

Place the butter in a basin and cook, using microwaves only, on high for $1\frac{1}{2}$ minutes to melt. Add the garlic, if using, the breadcrumbs, salt and cayenne to taste, mixing well. Add the buttered crumbs to the cooked sprouts and toss. Cook, uncovered, using microwaves only, on high for 3 minutes, stirring once. Serve hot.

RED CABBAGE CASSEROLE

SERVES 6

1 (1-kg/2-lb) red cabbage, cored and shredded
3 tablespoons apple juice or water
4 cooking apples, peeled, cored and chopped
pinch of ground cloves
1 tablespoon white wine vinegar
1 tablespoon brown sugar
1 tablespoon redcurrant jelly
25 g/1 oz butter

Place the red cabbage in a casserole dish with the apple juice or water and apple. Cover and cook, using microwaves only, on high for 12–14 minutes until tender, stirring once.

Stir in the cloves, wine vinegar, sugar, redcurrant jelly and butter, blending well. Cover and cook, using microwaves only, on high for 2 minutes.

Serve hot, with roasts, game, frankfurters or sausages.

LEMON AND GARLIC POTATOES

SERVES 4

20 g/$\frac{3}{4}$ oz butter
20 g/$\frac{3}{4}$ oz plain flour
450 ml/$\frac{3}{4}$ pint milk
2 tablespoons lemon juice
grated rind of $\frac{1}{2}$ lemon
1 clove garlic, crushed
salt and freshly ground black pepper
1 kg/2 lb potatoes, thinly sliced
chopped chives to garnish

Place the butter and flour in a basin, then whisk in the milk. Cook, using microwaves only, on high for 4–5 minutes.

Stir in the lemon juice and rind, garlic, salt and pepper. Place the potato slices in an ovenproof casserole dish, cover and cook, using microwaves only, on high for 7 minutes. Rearrange slightly, lifting some of the potato slices from the middle towards the outside. Then press down gently to neaten.

Pour over the sauce and cook at 200c using medium microwave setting for 20 minutes. Garnish with chopped chives. Serve hot with chops, steak or chicken.

Clockwise from bottom left: Crumbly Buttered Brussels; Red Cabbage Casserole; Lemon and Garlic Potatoes

CAULIFLOWER CHEESE SPECIAL

SERVES 4

1 small cauliflower, trimmed and cut into
  florets
8 tablespoons cold water
175 g/6 oz quick-cooking macaroni
600 ml/1 pint boiling water
175 g/6 oz rindless streaky bacon, chopped
25 g/1 oz butter
25 g/1 oz plain flour
350 ml/12 fl oz milk
2 teaspoons chive mustard
salt and freshly ground black pepper
75 g/3 oz Cheddar cheese, grated

Garnish
tomato slices
flat-leaf parsley sprigs

Place the cauliflower florets and water in a large bowl. Cover and cook, using microwaves only, on high for 10 minutes, stirring once. Drain thoroughly. Place the macaroni in a deep bowl with the boiling water. Cover and cook, using microwaves only, on high for 7 minutes. Allow to stand for 3 minutes, then drain thoroughly.

Put the bacon in a basin and cook, using microwaves only, on high for 4 minutes, stirring once. Drain thoroughly on absorbent kitchen paper. Place the butter in a large basin or jug and cook, using microwaves only, on high for $\frac{1}{2}$ minute to melt. Add the flour, blending well. Gradually add the milk and cook, using microwaves only, on high for 4–5 minutes, stirring every 1 minute until smooth and thickened. Stir in the chive mustard, salt and pepper to taste and cheese until melted.

Toss the cauliflower florets, macaroni and bacon in the sauce and spoon into a serving dish. Cook, using microwaves only, on high for 2–3 minutes, then serve, garnished with tomato slices and parsley sprigs.

BROCCOLI AND CHICKEN BAKE

SERVES 4–6

350 g/12 oz broccoli spears, trimmed
4 tablespoons water
pinch of salt
225 g/8 oz cooked chicken, cut into thin strips
1 small onion, halved
1 carrot, sliced
1 bay leaf
12 peppercorns
few parsley sprigs
300 ml/$\frac{1}{2}$ pint milk
25 g/1 oz butter
25 g/1 oz plain flour
freshly ground black pepper
50 g/2 oz toasted flaked almonds to garnish

Place the broccoli spears in a shallow dish with the water and salt, arranging the stalks round the outside of the dish and the florets in the centre. Cover and cook, using microwaves only, on high for 6 minutes. Drain thoroughly. Add the chicken and mix well.

Place the onion, carrot, bay leaf, peppercorns, parsley and milk in a large jug. Cook, using microwaves only, on defrost for 10–11 minutes until hot. Strain. Place the butter in a jug or basin and cook, using microwaves only, on high for $\frac{1}{2}$ minute to melt. Stir in the flour and salt and pepper to taste. Gradually add the strained milk and cook, using microwaves only, on high for 2–3 minutes, stirring once, until smooth and thickened. Whisk well, then pour over the broccoli and chicken mixture.

Cover and cook, using microwaves only, on high for 3–4 minutes, turning the dish twice. Sprinkle with the almonds and serve at once.

Clockwise from top left: Cauliflower Cheese Special; Broccoli and Chicken Bake; Stuffed Peppers

STUFFED PEPPERS

SERVES 6

1 tablespoon oil
1 onion, chopped
450 g/1 lb minced beef
5 tablespoons beef stock
1 tablespoon tomato purée
100 g/4 oz button mushrooms, chopped
salt and freshly ground black pepper
2 medium red peppers
2 medium green peppers
2 medium yellow peppers
1 (450-g/1-lb) can baked beans in tomato
sauce
1 (225-g/8-oz) can chopped tomatoes
1 clove garlic, crushed
1 teaspoon dried mixed herbs
rosemary sprigs to garnish

Place the oil and onion in a large bowl. Cover and cook, using microwaves only, on high for 3 minutes. Stir in the beef, breaking up the meat well. Cook, using microwaves only, on high for 9 minutes, stirring and breaking up the beef twice. Add the stock, tomato purée, mushroom and salt and pepper to taste. Cover and cook, using microwaves only, on high for 8 minutes, stirring once.

Meanwhile, cut a slice from the top of each pepper. Remove core and seeds. Place the peppers in a bowl, cover and cook, using microwaves only, on high for 4½ minutes, turn over and cook for 4½ minutes.

Combine the meat mixture with the beans. Stand the peppers upright in a shallow dish and fill with the bean and beef mixture. Mix the tomatoes with the garlic and herbs and spoon around the peppers. Cover and cook at 200 c using medium microwave setting for 8–10 minutes. Garnish with rosemary sprigs and serve.

RATATOUILLE

SERVES 4

1 large aubergine, trimmed and cut into
  chunks
salt and freshly ground black pepper
50 ml/2 fl oz olive oil
1 red pepper, deseeded and chopped
1 large onion, chopped
2 cloves garlic, crushed
225 g/8 oz courgettes, sliced
450 g/1 lb tomatoes, peeled and roughly
  chopped
plenty of chopped parsley

Place the aubergine in a colander and sprinkle with
salt. Leave in the sink or over a draining board for
20–30 minutes, then rinse and dry. Place in a large
dish with the oil and mix in the red pepper, onion
and garlic.

Cover and cook, using microwaves only, on
high for 5 minutes, stir well, then cook on high for
a further 5 minutes. Stir in the courgette and
tomato, add some of the parsley and re-cover.
Cook for 5–8 minutes, or until all the vegetables
are cooked. Add seasoning to taste and extra
parsley. Serve at once.

COOKING VEGETABLES USING MICROWAVES ONLY

Vegetable	Cooking time in minutes on high	Cooking instructions
Artichokes, globe –4 –2 –1	20–25 15–17 8–10	Wash and trim off stalk. Snip off leaf tips. Shake off excess water and put in roasting bag. Secure opening loosely with elastic band. Turn halfway through cooking. Leave to stand for 5 minutes, remove centre leaves and hairy choke from middle. Serve hot or cold.
Artichokes, Jerusalem 450 g/1 lb	10–12	Peel and place in dish with 3 tablespoons water and a little lemon juice. Cover and rearrange halfway through cooking. Leave to stand for 2 minutes, then serve with butter and snipped chives.
Asparagus 450 g/1 lb	5–7	Trim off woody stalk ends and wash. Put in roasting bag, secure end loosely with elastic band and rearrange halfway through cooking. Snip off corner of bag and drain over sink or bowl. Stand 3–4 minutes before serving.
Beans, broad 450 g/1 lb shelled weight	7–9	Put in dish with 2 tablespoons water. Cover and stir halfway through cooking. Stand 3 minutes before serving.
Beans, French or runner 450 g/1 lb	6–8	Put beans in dish with 2 tablespoons water. Cover and rearrange halfway through cooking. Stand for 3 minutes before serving.
Beetroot 450 g/1 lb	8–10	Wash and trim; do not peel. Put in dish with 2 tablespoons water. Cover and rearrange halfway through cooking.
Broccoli 450 g/1 lb	7–8	Put in dish with 2 tablespoons water. Cover and rearrange halfway through cooking. Stand 3 minutes before serving.

Vegetable	Cooking time in minutes on high	Cooking instructions
Brussels sprouts 450 g/1 lb	8–10	Put in dish with 2 tablespoons water. Rearrange halfway through cooking.
Cabbage –Savoy type 450 g/1 lb	8–10	Shred, put in dish with 3 tablespoons water. Cover and rearrange halfway through cooking.
–white	10–15	As above; timing depends on required cooked texture.
Carrots 225 g/8 oz	5–6	Trim and cut into matchstick strips. Rinse, drain and put in dish with knob of butter, $\frac{1}{2}$ teaspoon sugar and 1 tablespoon water. Rearrange halfway through cooking. Sprinkle with chopped parsley and serve.
Cauliflower –whole (about 450 g/ 1 lb)	12–15	Trim, wash and shake off water. Place in dish and cover. Stand for 3 minutes before serving.
–florets (about 225 g/ 8 oz)	5–6	Wash and place in dish or roasting bag. Secure end loosely with elastic band or cover and rearrange halfway through cooking.
Celeriac (1 kg/2 lb)	15–17	Peel, trim and cut into cubes. Wash and put in dish with 4 tablespoons water. Rearrange halfway through cooking.
Corn-on-the-cob –2 cobs –4 cobs	7–8 15–16	Trim cobs, removing all husk. Put in roasting bag with 2 tablespoons water. Stand 2 minutes before serving.
Courgettes 225 g/8 oz	3–5	Trim and slice. Place in dish with knob of butter. Cover and rearrange halfway through cooking.
Leeks 450 g/1 lb	5–7	Trim and slice. Wash well, shake off excess water but leave wet. Place in dish and cover. Stir halfway through cooking.
Marrow 450 g/1 lb	8–10	Peel and cut into cubes. Put in dish with 2 tablespoons water. Cover and rearrange halfway through cooking. Stand 3 minutes before serving.
Mushrooms, button (whole) 225 g/8 oz	2–3	Put in dish with generous knob of butter and cover. Stir halfway through cooking and serve sprinkled with chopped parsley.
Onions, 4 large whole	10–12	Place in dish with 2 tablespoons water and cover. Turn over halfway through cooking. Leave to stand for 5 minutes before draining and serving.
Parsnips 675 g/1½ lb	15–17	Peel and cut into chunks. Put in dish with 4 tablespoons water. Stand 3 minutes before draining and mashing with butter and seasoning.
Peas 450 g/1 lb shelled weight	7–10	Wash and place in dish with 2 tablespoons water. Cover and stir halfway through cooking. Serve drained, dotted with butter.
Potatoes –new 450 g/ 1 lb	5	Scrub and wash, then put in dish with 2 tablespoons water. Stand 3 minutes before serving.
–new 1 kg/ 2 lb	10–12	As above.
–old, cubed, 1 kg/2 lb	15–18	Peel and cube. Put in dish with 4 tablespoons water. Mash before serving.
baked 1 –2 –3 –4	8 12–15 20–22 25–28	Scrub well, cut out eyes. Prick skin and put on double-thick layer of absorbent kitchen paper. Turn and rearrange halfway through cooking.
Spinach 450 g/1 lb 1 kg/2 lb	5–6 10–12	Wash and shred (if liked). Shake off excess water and put in dish. Cover and stir halfway through cooking.
Spring greens 450 g/1 lb	7–10	Trim and shred. Place in dish with 3 tablespoons water. Stand 3 minutes. Drain, serve with butter.
Swede 675 g/1½ lb	15–17	Peel and cut into cubes. Put in dish with 3 tablespoons water. Stand 3 minutes before draining. Mash with butter and pepper.

Supper Dishes and Snacks

KEDGEREE

SERVES 4

1 onion, chopped
25 g/1 oz butter
grated rind of 1 lemon
½ teaspoon turmeric
pinch of curry powder
225 g/8 oz long-grain rice
600 ml/1 pint boiling water
salt and freshly ground black pepper
450 g/1 lb smoked haddock, skinned and cut
   into chunks
2 tablespoons chopped parsley
4 hard-boiled eggs, roughly chopped
parsley sprigs to garnish

Put the onion and butter in a casserole dish and cook, using microwaves only, on high for 3 minutes. Stir in the lemon rind, spices and rice. Pour in the water and add seasoning. Cover and cook, using microwaves only, on high for 10 minutes.

Stir lightly, then add the fish, without stirring it in, and re-cover the dish. Cook on high for a further 5–10 minutes, or until the fish is cooked and the majority of the water absorbed. Stir in the parsley and eggs and serve, garnished with parsley sprigs.

Additional ingredients
You may like to try using the following ingredients, some to replace certain items, others to add to the dish.

Use smoked mackerel instead of smoked haddock, adding it 5 minutes before the end of the cooking time. Add 50 g/2 oz roughly chopped salted peanuts. Add 50 g/2 oz sultanas, raisins or currants. Omit the spices and cook with a bay leaf; remove the bay leaf before serving. Add 100 g/4 oz sliced mushrooms.

PIZZA

SERVES 2-4

Base
100 g/4 oz strong white flour
salt and freshly ground black pepper
2 teaspoons easy-blend dried yeast or ordinary
    dried yeast
50 ml/2 fl oz lukewarm water
1 tablespoon oil

Topping
1 large onion, chopped
1 tablespoon oil
2 cloves garlic, crushed
½ teaspoon dried marjoram
1 (400-g/14-oz) can tomatoes
1 tablespoon capers, roughly chopped
    (optional)
salt and freshly ground black pepper
175 g/6 oz mozzarella cheese, cubed
10–12 black olives, stoned (optional)

Put the flour in a bowl and add a pinch of salt. Stir in the easy-blend dried yeast. If using ordinary dried yeast, then sprinkle it over the lukewarm water and leave in a warm place until the yeast has dissolved and the liquid is frothy. Add the oil and water or yeast liquid to the flour and mix together to make a soft dough.

Turn the dough out on to a lightly floured surface and knead thoroughly until very smooth and elastic. Lightly flour the bowl, put the dough in it and cover with a damp cloth or a piece of cling film. Leave in a warm place until doubled in size.

Meanwhile, prepare the topping. Put the onion, oil and garlic in a basin and cook, using microwaves only, on high for 3 minutes. Stir in the marjoram.

Lightly grease a 25-cm/10-in flan dish. Turn the risen dough out on to a lightly floured surface and knead it very briefly. Roll it out into a circle to fit the base of the dish. Lift the dough into the dish, pressing it into the corners but not up the sides. Spread the onion mixture evenly over the dough, then top with the tomatoes and sprinkle with the capers, if using. Season with a little salt and plenty of pepper. Top with the mozzarella and the olives, if using, distributing both evenly over the pizza.

Bake the pizza at 250 c using medium microwave setting for 10–12 minutes, or until the top is bubbling and lightly browned and the edges are brown and crisp. Serve freshly cooked, with a green salad.

Pizza Toppings

Each of the following toppings is to go over the basic onion, garlic and marjoram mixture used in the main recipe.

Mushroom Pizza Add 225 g/8 oz thinly sliced button mushrooms and top with the mozzarella as in the main recipe. Sprinkle with a little chopped parsley – if you like – before serving.

Mixed Vegetable Pizza Add 1 chopped green pepper to the onion mixture before cooking. Top with canned artichoke hearts, a few sliced button mushrooms, 1 small sliced courgette and 100 g/4 oz thinly sliced tomatoes. You will be clever to balance any more than 100 g/4 oz thinly sliced mozzarella cheese on top!

Salami and Tomato Pizza Top with 100 g/4 oz salami, then add the tomatoes and mozzarella with olives as in the main recipe.

Bacon and Pepper Pizza Add 2 chopped green or red peppers to the onion mixture before cooking. Chop 225 g/8 oz rindless lean bacon and sprinkle it over the pizza. Top with 100 g/4 oz chopped tomatoes and 100 g/4 oz diced mozzarella.

Tuna and Tomato Pizza Add 1 (198-g/7-oz) can tuna, drained and flaked, and 225 g/8 oz chopped tomatoes. Top with the mozzarella and olives as in the main recipe.

CREAM CHEESE FLAN

SERVES 4

Shortcrust Pastry
175 g/6 oz plain flour
pinch of salt
75 g/3 oz margarine
2 tablespoons cold water

Filling
225 g/8 oz low-fat soft cheese, for example,
   quark or curd cheese
100 g/4 oz Cheddar cheese, grated
100 g/4 oz cooked ham, diced
3 eggs
300 ml/½ pint milk
salt and freshly ground black pepper
a little grated nutmeg

Sift the flour and salt into a bowl. Cut the margarine into small pieces and rub into the flour until the mixture resembles fine breadcrumbs. Add sufficient water to mix to a soft dough. On a lightly floured surface, roll out the pastry to a circle large enough to line a 20-cm/8-in flan dish. Prick the pastry all over, then chill.

Meanwhile prepare the filling. Mash the cheeses together with a fork, then mix in the ham. Beat together the eggs and milk, add seasoning to taste and a little nutmeg. Combine with the cheese and ham mixture. Cook the empty flan case at 220 c using medium microwave setting for 3 minutes.

Pour the filling into the flan case and bake at 220 c using medium microwave setting for 15 minutes, or until golden.

TOMATO FLAN

SERVES 4

1 quantity shortcrust pastry, using
   wholemeal flour, if liked (left)
1 onion, finely chopped
2 cloves garlic, crushed
1 tablespoon oil
1 (400-g/14-oz) can chopped tomatoes
1 tablespoon tomato purée
4 tablespoons grated Parmesan cheese
pinch of oregano
salt and freshly ground black pepper
4 stuffed olives, sliced

On a lightly floured surface, roll out the pastry to a circle large enough to line a 20-cm/8-in flan dish. Prick the pastry all over, then chill for 15 minutes.

For the filling, put the onion in a large basin with the garlic and oil. Cook, using microwaves only, on high for 3 minutes. Add the tomatoes, tomato purée, 3 tablespoons of the Parmesan, the oregano and salt and pepper to taste. Cook, using microwaves only, on high for 5 minutes.

Cook the empty flan case at 250 c using medium microwave setting for 3 minutes. Spoon the tomato filling into the flan case, add the olives, then bake at 220 c using medium microwave setting for 10–12 minutes, or until golden.

SALAMI QUICHE

SERVES 6

1 quantity shortcrust pastry (left)
1 onion, chopped · 25 g/1 oz butter
3 tablespoons plain flour
300 ml/½ pint milk
100 g/4 oz mushrooms, sliced
1 egg · 50 g/2 oz salami

On a lightly floured surface, roll out the pastry to a circle large enough to line a 23-cm/9-in flan dish. Prick the pastry all over, then chill for 15 minutes.

For the filling, cook the onion and butter in a basin, using microwaves only, on high for 3 minutes. Whisk in the 3 tablespoons flour and the milk. Cook, using microwaves only, on high for 3–4 minutes. Whisk well until smooth. Whisk in the mushrooms and egg. Bake the pastry case blind at 220 c using medium microwave setting for 5 minutes. Remove the beans, then pour in the filling. Top with the salami and bake at 220 c using medium microwave setting for 8–9 minutes.

QUICHE LORRAINE

SERVES 6

1 quantity shortcrust pastry (page 48)

Filling
2 onions, chopped
175 g/6 oz rindless bacon, roughly chopped
100 g/4 oz Emmental cheese
3 eggs
300 ml/½ pint single cream or milk
salt and freshly ground black pepper

Turn the pastry out on to a lightly floured surface and roll out into a circle large enough to line a 25-cm/10-in flan dish. Lift the pastry into the dish and trim off any excess by rolling the rolling pin over the edge of the dish. Prick the base all over, then chill. For the filling, put the onion and bacon in a basin and cook, using microwaves only, on high for 5 minutes.

When the pastry has chilled for about 15–20 minutes, bake it at 250 c (without preheating the oven) using medium microwave setting for 5 minutes. Remove from the oven and re-set the temperature to 200 c.

Sprinkle the onion and bacon mixture into the quiche, then add the cheese. Beat the eggs with the cream or milk and add seasoning to taste. Pour this mixture into the quiche and bake at 200 c using medium microwave setting for 12–15 minutes, or until the quiche is lightly browned. Serve hot or warm.

MACARONI MINCE

SERVES 4–6

1 onion, chopped
2 cloves garlic, crushed
1 green pepper, deseeded and chopped
2 tablespoons oil
450 g/1 lb minced beef
1 (400-g/14-oz) can chopped tomatoes
150 ml/¼ pint boiling beef stock
salt and freshly ground black pepper
½ teaspoon dried basil
175 g/6 oz macaroni

Sauce
50 g/2 oz butter or margarine
50 g/2 oz plain flour
600 ml/1 pint milk
100 g/4 oz Cheddar cheese, grated

Topping
50 g/2 oz salted peanuts, chopped
2 tablespoons grated Parmesan cheese

Place the onion, garlic, pepper and oil in a large basin and cook, using microwaves only, on high for 5 minutes. Stir in the minced beef and cook for a further 5 minutes. Add the tomatoes, stock, seasoning and basil, then turn the mixture into an ovenproof dish.

Cook the pasta conventionally, in plenty of boiling salted water, for 12–15 minutes until tender. Drain.

Whisk the sauce ingredients together in a large basin, then cook, using microwaves only, on high for 8–10 minutes, or until boiling and thickened. Stir in the macaroni, pour over the meat, then sprinkle with the peanuts and Parmesan.

Cook at 220 c using medium microwave setting for 15–20 minutes, until browned on top and cooked through.

STUFFED MINCE ROLL

SERVES 4

50 g/2 oz rice
250 ml/8 fl oz boiling water
1 onion, chopped
1 clove garlic, crushed
25 g/1 oz butter
675 g/1½ lb minced beef
1 teaspoon Worcestershire sauce
2 tablespoons chopped parsley
1 egg, lightly beaten
salt and freshly ground black pepper
100 g/4 oz mozzarella cheese,
  thinly sliced
1 teaspoon basil

Put the rice and water in a basin, cover and cook, using microwaves only, on high for 15 minutes, or until the water has been absorbed. Place the onion and garlic in a basin with the butter. Cook, using microwaves only, on high for 3 minutes.

Mix with the minced beef, Worcestershire sauce, parsley, rice, egg and seasoning. Pound thoroughly with a wooden spoon, making sure the ingredients are well mixed. Turn out on to a piece of greased greaseproof paper and press flat to form a 23 × 33-cm/9 × 13-in rectangle. Top with the mozzarella and basil. Roll up like a traditional Swiss roll, patting it neatly into shape. Place on a greased flan dish. Cook at 200 c using medium microwave setting for 20 minutes. Serve sliced into eight portions on a serving dish, with tomato sauce (see recipe page 62) poured over, if liked.

RASPBERRY DELIGHT

SERVES 4

350 g/12 oz raspberries, defrosted if frozen
2 tablespoons sugar
100 g/4 oz low-fat soft cheese, for example,
  curd cheese or sieved cottage cheese
1 tablespoon honey
3–4 tablespoons single cream
grated rind of $\frac{1}{2}$ lemon
150 g/5 oz desiccated coconut
25 g/1 oz plain wholemeal flour
25 g/1 oz soft brown sugar
50 g/2 oz butter, melted

Place the raspberries in a deep dish. Sprinkle the sugar over the fruit, then cook, using microwaves only, on high for 2 minutes.

Mix together the cheese, honey, cream and lemon rind. Spread the mixture over the fruit. Combine the remaining ingredients and spread over the cheese mixture to cover it completely.

Bake at 220 c using medium microwave setting for 8 minutes, or until golden and hot through. Allow the Raspberry Delight to stand for 5 minutes before serving.

Desserts

Apart from Crème Caramel, each of the desserts in the chapter benefits from the combination cooking method.

APPLE CHARLOTTE

SERVES 4

4 slices bread, crusts removed
25 g/1 oz demerara sugar
pinch each of ground cinnamon and cloves
75 ml/3 fl oz orange juice

Fruit base
450 g/1 lb cooking apples
50 g/2 oz demerara sugar
50 g/2 oz butter

Cut the bread into neat dice. Mix the sugar with spices and orange juice in a basin. Cook, using microwaves only, on high for 1–2 minutes until the sugar has dissolved. Stir well, then pour over the bread and set aside.

Peel, core and slice the apples. Place in an ovenproof dish with the sugar. Top with the soaked bread, taking care not to break up the dice. Pour over any remaining syrup and dot with butter. Cook at 200 c using medium microwave setting for 10 minutes, or until golden brown and crunchy on top.

Top: Raspberry Delight; *bottom*: Apple Charlotte

AUTUMN CRUMBLE

SERVES 4

350 g/12 oz cooking apples, peeled, cored and sliced
225 g/8 oz blackberries, cleaned and hulled
50 g/2 oz sugar

Topping
75 g/3 oz plain flour
50 g/2 oz butter
50 g/2 oz sugar
25 g/1 oz ground almonds

Place the fruit in a large dish and sprinkle with the sugar. Mix lightly, then press down gently with the back of a spoon.

Sift the flour into a bowl, rub in the butter until the mixture resembles fine breadcrumbs. Stir in the sugar and almonds and sprinkle this topping over the fruit.

Bake at 220 c using medium microwave setting for 8–10 minutes, until golden brown. Serve the crumble with custard, cream or vanilla ice cream.

Cook's Tip
Instead of the ground almonds in the topping, you may like to try a handful of breakfast cereal for a crunchy texture. Do not weigh out 25 g/1 oz of a lightweight cereal or there will be far too much! Try a bran-based cereal or those flaked cereals that are made from oats and other ingredients.

QUEEN OF PUDDINGS

SERVES 6

100 g/4 oz fresh white breadcrumbs
4 eggs
175 g/6 oz sugar
grated rind of 1 lemon
a little grated nutmeg
600 ml/1 pint milk
6–8 tablespoons apricot, raspberry or strawberry jam, as preferred

Grease a 23-cm/9-in dish. Place the breadcrumbs in the dish. Separate two of the eggs; put the yolks in a bowl and set the whites aside. Add the whole eggs to the yolks. Beat in 50 g/2 oz of the sugar, the lemon rind and nutmeg. Gradually pour in the milk, then pour the mixture into the dish over the breadcrumbs. Press down with a fork and set aside for 15 minutes.

Bake at 180 c using medium microwave setting for 6–8 minutes, or until almost set. Remove from the oven and allow to stand for 5 minutes.

Spread the jam over the pudding. Whisk the egg whites until they stand in stiff peaks, then use a metal spoon to fold in the remaining sugar. Spread the meringue over the pudding, forking it into peaks. Bake at 250 c using medium microwave setting for about 3 minutes to lightly brown the meringue. If the meringue is not browned after 3 minutes, then continue cooking using just convection setting – do not use microwaves any longer or the meringue will overcook before browning. Serve freshly cooked.

Top: Autumn Crumble; *bottom*: Queen of Puddings

CRÈME CARAMEL

SERVES 4

Caramel
100 g/4 oz sugar
4 tablespoons water

Custard
2 small eggs
5 teaspoons sugar
350 ml/12 fl oz milk
a few drops of vanilla essence

Put the sugar and water in a basin and cook, using microwaves only, on high for 2 minutes. Stir well, then continue to cook on high for a further 9–11 minutes, or until the caramel is a pale golden colour. Take care that the caramel does not overcook and watch it closely towards the end of the time.

Divide the caramel between four ramekins. Hold them with an oven glove or tea-towel and swirl the caramel round the sides. Set aside.

Beat the eggs with the sugar, then add the milk and vanilla essence. Strain into the dishes. Stand the ramekins in a flan dish, then put it in the oven and pour boiling water to come halfway up the flan dish. Cook, using microwaves only, on high for 3–3½ minutes. The custard should be very lightly set. Turn the dishes once during cooking. Cool, then chill overnight. Turn out on to individual plates and serve.

TARTE TATIN

SERVES 6

Pastry
225 g/8 oz plain flour
175 g/6 oz butter or margarine
50 g/2 oz ground almonds
25 g/1 oz sugar
2 egg yolks

Filling
butter to grease
10–12 small dessert apples, peeled and cored
juice of 1 lemon
75 g/3 oz sugar
4 tablespoons water

Sift the flour into a bowl, then rub in the butter. Stir in the almonds and sugar and work in the egg yolks to bind the pastry dough.

Heat the oven to 220 c. Grease a 23-cm/9-in flan dish generously with the butter. Place the whole apples in the dish, packing them in neatly.

Sprinkle over the lemon juice. Roll out the pastry to a circle slightly larger than the dish. Lift the pastry over the apples and tuck the edges into the dish. Chill for 30 minutes. Cook at 220 c using medium microwave setting for 13–15 minutes, until the pastry is cooked and lightly browned.

Leave to stand for 5 minutes. Place the sugar and water in a heatproof glass jug or basin. Cook, using microwaves only, on high for 7–10 minutes, or until a pale caramel forms. Stir the syrup after 5 minutes and watch it closely for the remaining cooking time to ensure that it does not overcook. Gently ease the pastry edges away from the dish. Place a large plate on top of the pastry and invert the tart on to the plate. Drizzle the caramel over the apples, then serve with cream.

Note Instead of making a caramel to coat the apples you may like to spoon clear honey over them.

APRICOT CUSTARD TART

SERVES 6–8

Pastry
175 g/6 oz plain flour
100 g/4 oz butter or margarine
25 g/1 oz sugar
grated rind of 1 orange
1 tablespoon water
1 egg yolk

Filling
2 (425-g/15-oz) cans apricots, drained
grated rind of 1 lemon
25 g/1 oz sugar
2 large eggs
450 ml/¾ pint milk

Heat the oven to 180 c. Put the flour in a bowl and rub in the butter or margarine until the mixture resembles coarse breadcrumbs. Stir in the sugar and orange rind, then mix in the water and egg yolk to make a soft pastry dough. Chill for 5 minutes.

Roll out the pastry on a lightly floured surface into a circle large enough to line a 23-cm/9-in flan dish. Trim off the excess pastry by rolling the rolling pin round the rim of the dish. Prick the base and chill for 15 minutes. Place a piece of greaseproof paper in the pastry case and sprinkle a handful of baking beans or dried peas over it. Bake at 180 c using medium microwave setting for 7 minutes.

Remove the paper and beans and allow the pastry to cool slightly, then arrange the apricot halves in the base. Beat the lemon rind, sugar and eggs together, then gradually beat in the milk. Strain the mixture through a fine sieve into the flan. Bake at 180 c using medium microwave setting for 12–15 minutes, or until the custard has set. Cool. Serve cold, with single cream if you like.

Baking

In this chapter you will find that the results you missed when baking by microwaves only are fully achieved.

CHERRY AND ALMOND CAKE

MAKES 1 18-cm/7-in CAKE

225 g/8 oz glacé cherries
175 g/6 oz butter or margarine
175 g/6 oz sugar
3 eggs
$\frac{1}{4}$ teaspoon almond essence
200 g/7 oz self-raising flour
100 g/4 oz blanched almonds, chopped
2 tablespoons milk

Line an 18-cm/7-in deep, round dish with greaseproof paper and grease the paper thoroughly. Halve the cherries, put them in a sieve and wash them under warm water. Drain the fruit and dry it on absorbent kitchen paper. Set aside.

Beat the butter or margarine and sugar together until very pale and creamy. Beat in the eggs and almond essence, adding a little of the flour if the mixture begins to curdle. Add a little flour to the cherries and toss them in it to coat them completely. Fold the remaining flour into the cake mixture using a metal spoon. Fold in the cherries, then fold in the almonds and milk.

Turn the mixture into the prepared dish and lightly smooth the top. Bake at 220 c using medium microwave setting for 13–15 minutes, or until the cake has risen and lightly browned. Leave the cake in the dish for a few minutes, then turn it out on to a wire rack to cool. Remove the paper when the cake has cooled completely.

Clockwise from top right: Cherry and Almond Cake; Dundee Cake; Upside-down Cake

DUNDEE CAKE

MAKES 1 18-cm/7-in CAKE

175 g/6 oz butter or margarine
175 g/6 oz sugar
3 eggs
200 g/7 oz self-raising flour
350 g/12 oz mixed dried fruit
100 g/4 oz blanched almonds, chopped,
    plus 50 g/2 oz whole blanched almonds
4 tablespoons sherry

Heat the oven to 180 c. Line an 18-cm/7-in deep, round dish with greaseproof paper and grease the paper thoroughly. The paper should stand about 2.5 cm/1 in above the rim of the dish.

Beat the butter or margarine and sugar together until very pale and creamy. Beat in the eggs, adding a little of the flour if the mixture begins to curdle. Sprinkle a spoonful of the flour over the dried fruit and mix well. Add the rest of the flour to the creamed mixture and fold it in very lightly using a metal spoon. Sprinkle in the fruit and chopped nuts, then fold these ingredients in using the metal spoon. Lastly, fold in the sherry.

Turn the mixture into the prepared dish and lightly smooth the top. Top with concentric circles of almonds. Bake at 180 c using medium microwave setting for 20–22 minutes, or until the cake has risen and lightly browned on top. Leave the cake in the dish for a few minutes, then turn it out on to a wire rack to cool. Remove the paper when the cake has cooled completely.

UPSIDE-DOWN CAKE

SERVES 6–8

1 (425-g/15-oz) can pear halves, drained
3–4 glacé cherries, halved
100 g/4 oz butter, softened, or soft margarine
100 g/4 oz sugar
2 eggs
100 g/4 oz self-raising flour
$\frac{1}{2}$ teaspoon baking powder
1 teaspoon ground mixed spice
50 g/2 oz walnuts, finely chopped
2 tablespoons milk
2 tablespoons clear honey

Heat the oven to 200 c. Base-line and grease an oblong dish – about 20 × 13 cm/8 × 5 in. Alternatively use an 18-cm/7-in deep, round dish.

Arrange the pear halves in the dish: put a glacé cherry half in each of the core cavities, then turn

the pears cut side down. Put all the remaining ingredients, except the honey, in a bowl and beat vigorously until very soft and creamy, and pale in colour. Spoon this mixture into the dish over the pears. Spread evenly, then bake at 200c using medium microwave setting for 13–15 minutes, or until the cake is set, risen and browned on top. Leave to stand for 10 minutes.

Place the honey in a basin and warm, using microwaves only, on high for 30 seconds. Turn the pudding out on to a serving platter and ease away the lining paper; (use a pointed knife to slide the cherries off the paper, if they stick to it). Brush with honey and serve hot, cut into individual portions.

Cook's Tip
Use the syrup from the pears to make a delicious sauce to serve with the Upside-down Cake. Stir into 1 tablespoon cornflour, add the grated rind of 1 orange and cook, using microwaves only, on high for 3–5 minutes, until boiling and thickened.

ORANGE GÂTEAU

MAKES 1 18-cm/7-in CAKE

175 g/6 oz butter or margarine
175 g/6 oz sugar
grated rind of 1 orange
3 eggs
175 g/6 oz self-raising flour
1 teaspoon baking powder
100 g/4 oz ground almonds
75 ml/3 fl oz orange juice

Filling and Decoration
300 ml/½ pint double cream
2 tablespoons icing sugar
grated rind and juice of 1 orange
fresh orange segments

Heat the oven to 200 c. Line and grease an 18-cm/7-in deep, round dish. Beat the butter or margarine and sugar with the orange rind until very pale and creamy. Beat in the eggs, adding a little of the flour if the mixture begins to curdle. Sift the flour with the baking powder. Fold these dry ingredients into the creamed mixture using a metal spoon, then fold in the ground almonds. Fold in the orange juice.

Turn the mixture into the prepared dish and smooth the top. Bake at 200 c using medium microwave setting for 12–15 minutes, or until the cake is well risen and firm on top. Leave the cake in the dish for 10 minutes, then transfer it to a wire rack to cool. Remove the paper when the cake has cooled completely.

When the cake is cold, slice it horizontally in half. Whip the cream and icing sugar with the orange rind and juice until the mixture stands in soft peaks. Sandwich the cake with a little of the cream. Spread the orange cream thinly over the top and sides of the cake.

Decorate with fresh orange segments and the remaining orange cream piped in swirls as shown.

Cook's Tip
Instead of ground almonds, grind desiccated coconut to a fine powder in a food processor or liquidiser.

BREAD

MAKES 1 LARGE LOAF OR 2 SMALL LOAVES

450 g/1 lb strong white or wholemeal flour
1 teaspoon salt
1 teaspoon sugar
50 g/2 oz margarine
1 sachet easy-blend dried yeast or 3 teaspoons ordinary dried yeast
300 ml/½ pint lukewarm water

Line a 1-kg/2-lb loaf dish with greaseproof paper and grease the paper thoroughly. The paper should stand above the rim of the dish by 2.5 cm/1 in, but it should not be too high.

Place the flour, salt and sugar in a bowl. Rub in the margarine and stir in the easy-blend yeast. If using ordinary dried yeast, then sprinkle it over the lukewarm water and leave in a warm place until the yeast has dissolved and the mixture is frothy.

Make a well in the dry ingredients and pour in the water or yeast liquid. Gradually stir in the flour to make a stiff dough. Use your hand to mix the last of the flour into the dough. Turn the dough out on to a lightly floured surface and knead it until very smooth and elastic. This first kneading should take about 10 minutes. Lightly flour the bowl and put the dough back into it. Cover with a damp cloth or a piece of cling film and leave in a warm place until doubled in size.

Turn the risen dough out on to a lightly floured surface and knead it briefly to knock out the gas. Press the dough into the prepared dish and cover with a dampened cloth or a piece of cling film. Leave in a warm place until the dough is well risen – it should stand above the rim of the dish.

Brush the dough with a little water and bake at 250 c using medium microwave setting for 10–12 minutes, or until the loaf is browned on top. Leave in the dish for a few minutes, then turn the bread out on to a wire rack to cool and remove the paper. The base of the bread will not be brown, but the top should be brown and crusty and, of course, the loaf should be cooked through.

Note
This recipe gives the basic technique for making dough for breads and buns. If you do not have a suitable 1-kg/2-lb loaf dish, use an 18–23-cm/7–9-in deep round dish instead. Alternatively, make two 450-g/1-lb loaves and bake as in the main recipe but for about 9 minutes. A 15-cm/6-in soufflé dish can be substituted for a small loaf dish.

Sauces

Microwaves only are used for sauce-making in this chapter – the ideal method for achieving speedy results.

BÉCHAMEL SAUCE

MAKES 600 ml/1 PINT

40 g/1½ oz plain flour
600 ml/1 pint milk
bay leaf
blade of mace
salt and freshly ground black pepper
knob of butter

Put the flour in a basin large enough to allow room for the sauce to boil up as it cooks. Gradually whisk in the milk, making sure that the mixture is smooth. Add the bay leaf and mace, seasoning and butter. Cook, using microwaves only, on high for 3 minutes. Whisk thoroughly, then cook for a further 5 minutes and whisk again. Cook on high for a further 1–3 minutes, until the sauce has boiled and thickened. Whisk well to remove any lumps, then taste and adjust the seasoning before serving.

Variations
Omit the bay leaf and mace from the above recipe and add the following ingredients:
Parsley Sauce Add 4–6 tablespoons chopped parsley to the sauce just before serving. Serve with fish or boiled ham.
Cheese Sauce Add 100 g/4 oz grated matured Cheddar cheese and 2 teaspoons prepared mustard to the sauce about 3 minutes before the end of the cooking time. Whisk well, then finish cooking as above. Serve with fish, vegetables, eggs or pasta.
Egg Sauce Add 4 chopped hard-boiled eggs to the sauce at the end of the cooking time. Serve with fish, pasta or vegetables.

TOMATO SAUCE

MAKES 600 ml/1 PINT

1 onion, chopped
1 small carrot, chopped
1 celery stick, chopped
2 cloves garlic, crushed
25 g/1 oz butter or 2 tablespoons oil
bay leaf
salt and freshly ground black pepper
½ teaspoon dried thyme
2 (400-g/14-oz) cans chopped tomatoes
150 ml/¼ pint red wine

Put the onion, carrot and celery in a large basin with the garlic and butter or oil. Mix well, cover and cook, using microwaves only, on high for 5 minutes. Add the bay leaf and seasoning. Stir in the thyme and tomatoes, then pour in the red wine. Re-cover and cook, using microwaves only, on high for a further 8 minutes.

Blend the sauce in a liquidiser or press it through a fine sieve. Reheat, using microwaves only, on high for 2 minutes before serving.

Serve with fish, meat, vegetables, rice or pasta.

HOLLANDAISE SAUCE

SERVES 4

2 tablespoons lemon juice
1 tablespoon water
2 large egg yolks
salt and freshly ground black pepper
100 g/4 oz butter

Place the lemon juice and water in a basin. Cook, using microwaves only, on high for about 3–5 minutes. At the end of the cooking time the liquid should be reduced to about 1 tablespoon. The time will vary with the individual oven. Whisk in the egg yolks immediately the liquid is removed from the oven. Add a little seasoning and set aside.

Put the butter in a basin and heat, using microwaves only, on high for 2–2½ minutes until melted and quite hot. Whisking all the time, add the butter in a slow trickle to the egg yolks.

Cook, using microwaves only, on high for a further 30–60 seconds, stir well and serve at once.

APPLE SAUCE

SERVES 4–6

**450 g/1 lb cooking apples, peeled, cored and
sliced**
75 g/3 oz sugar
25 g/1 oz butter

Put the apples and sugar in a casserole dish or basin
and cover. Cook, using microwaves only, on high
for 5–7 minutes. Beat well, adding the butter.

Serve cold with roast pork, baked or boiled
ham, or roast goose.

BRANDY SAUCE

MAKES 600 ml/1 PINT

3 tablespoons cornflour
3 tablespoons sugar
450 ml/¾ pint milk · 150 ml/¼ pint brandy

In a basin mix the cornflour with the sugar and a
little of the milk until smooth. Gradually whisk in
the remaining milk and cook, using microwaves
only, on high for 5 minutes.

Whisk thoroughly, then cook, using microwaves only, on high for a further 4 minutes, or
until the sauce boils and thickens. Whisk thoroughly, then whisk in the brandy and heat, using
microwaves only, on high for 1 minute. Serve hot
with Christmas pudding, mince pies, steamed
puddings or baked puddings.

CUSTARD SAUCE

MAKES 600 ml/1 PINT

This is a compromise between a traditional egg
custard and custard made using just custard
powder.

2 tablespoons custard powder
2 egg yolks
2 tablespoons sugar
600 ml/1 pint milk

Mix the custard powder with the egg yolks and
sugar, adding just enough of the milk to make a
smooth, thick cream. Heat the rest of the milk in a
large basin, using microwaves only, on high for 4
minutes.

Whisking all the time, gradually pour the milk
on to the custard powder mixture. Pour the
custard back into the basin and cook, using
microwaves only, on high for 2–4 minutes,
whisking once during cooking. The custard
should be slightly thickened and smooth. Serve
hot with fruit pies and other puddings.

Above: A range of sauce ingredients

INDEX